Fabricating the Body

Fabricating the Body:
Effects of Obligation and Exchange
in Contemporary Discourse

Edited by

Sarah Himsel Burcon

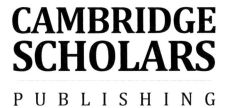

Fabricating the Body:
Effects of Obligation and Exchange in Contemporary Discourse,
Edited by Sarah Himsel Burcon

This book first published 2014

Cambridge Scholars Publishing

12 Back Chapman Street, Newcastle upon Tyne, NE6 2XX, UK

British Library Cataloguing in Publication Data
A catalogue record for this book is available from the British Library

ISBN (10): 1-4438-5232-5, ISBN (13): 978-1-4438-5232-6

This book is dedicated to my children:
Lucas, Jacob, and Nicole

TABLE OF CONTENTS

Section II: The Body in Popular Discourse

INTRODUCTION

SARAH HIMSEL BURCON AND CONTRIBUTORS

Fabricating the Body: Effects of Obligation and Exchange in Contemporary Discourse is comprised of nine chapters that revolve around the body, and specifically, portrayals of indebted bodies in literature and popular discourses. The first section, "The Body in Literature," examines issues related to gender and class, as well as human bonding and ethical concerns. Section two, "The Body in Popular Discourse," again, concerns gender in addition to matters related to marginalization. All of the chapters in some fashion explore identity and the body in cultural texts.

The Body in Literature

Chapter One, "A Paratactic 'Missing Link': Dorian Gray and the Performance of Embodied Modernity" by Rachel Herzl-Betz, traces Oscar Wilde's literary debt to the atavistic (the belief that humans could return to an earlier form of evolution) discourse of late-Victorian freak shows. It argues that, while critics have explored atavistic obligation in a range of *fin de siècle* texts, they have yet to connect the decadent movement with the ongoing popularity of performed abnormality. This chapter engages recent criticism in disability studies to follow the trappings and atavistic philosophy of the Victorian freak show that lives on in *The Picture of Dorian Gray* (1890-1).

Mr. Wroe's Virgins, a contemporary novel, is also set in 19th century England. Chapter Two, "A Gender in Debt: Labor and the Female Body in *Mr. Wroe's Virgins*" by Emily Workman Keller, explores the cultural landscape of Jane Rogers's novel and the effects that this culture had on Hannah, one of Rogers's protagonists. The chapter explores how Rogers's historical vantage influenced her creation of Hannah, a talented and hard-working woman whose labor is devalued because of her gender. To that end, the analysis juxtaposes 19th century and contemporary theoretical discourses, making use of two 19th century writers: Mary Wollstonecraft, author of *Vindication of the Rights of Woman*, a feminist manifesto; and

Anna Lætitia Barbauld, the poet who wrote "Washing-Day," a social satire concerned with the toils of domestic labor. The essay dwells upon the options available to single women in the early 19th century, and explores Hannah's characterization as the ideal female capable of navigating the changes that Rogers, by virtue of being able to look back at a time that has passed, is able to anticipate.

Chapters Three and Four also explore gender issues. Matthew J. Sherman's "The Costs of Debt: The Indebtedness of the Female Body in Arthur Schnitzler's *Fräulein Else*" examines the novella, *Fräulein Else,* which is the inner monologue of a nineteen year-old Viennese woman. The protagonist, Else, must decide if she will pose nude for Herr von Dorsday, who, in return, will pay off her father's substantial debt. Else contemplates the deed as her thoughts oscillate between repulsion and excitation. This chapter appropriates a psychoanalytic framework to uncover the reciprocity of external and internal realities, and to expose how psychical conflict, specifically regarding female sexuality and the body, reflects the interconnectedness of irreconcilable debts. This irreconcilability owes itself, to a great extent, to matters of gender and class. Else's body is the site for the negotiation of masculine desires. She is obligated to the patriarchal social structure that prostitutes her. There is no possibility for her to establish autonomy over her body or her sexuality. Her indebtedness denies reprieve and leads to a violent backlash against society and the self. In Chapter Four, "Unbinding the Tragic 'Dream' of Human Abjection: Paying the Debt of Gender-Based Abjection in Neil Gaiman's *The Sandman,*" Mary Catherine Harper points out how, as a whole, the linked volumes of *The Sandman* series explore the maturation and eventual tragic death of the central character, Morpheus. Furthermore, in the course of the ten plot-linked volumes, Morpheus shifts from allegorical figure to a well-rounded character that has to recognize, struggle to understand, and take responsibility for a range of human psycho-social problems in which he is implicated. As the chapter teases out Morpheus's struggle with his impulse to abjectify along gender lines, it exposes some of the tragic qualities of abjection still circulating in our postmodern cultural environment.

Moving away from gender and into the arena of a post-apocalyptic world, Chapter Five, Lo Chi Man's "The Land and the Human Body in McCarthy's *The Road*: The Importance of Moral Values in Human Connection and Bonding," examines Cormac McCarthy's *The Road* and argues that, as a post-apocalyptic fiction, it does not merely demonstrate the struggles of life in the state of devastation, but also forcefully leads the readers to reflect on the basis for the establishment of human bonding and the contribution to a meaningful life, as well as the fragility of moral values as illustrated through the connection between the catastrophic landscape and the human body. Under the context of the obliteration of the fundamental principles—the principles which are constructed by divine and authoritative governance regarding the moral standards and the meanings of human life—which indicates that the original developed systems and ideas of human civilization in the pre-apocalyptic world have been lost after the catastrophic incident, McCarthy actually provides the possibility of and hope for the recreation or reestablishment of human bonding, as well as raises the basis for a meaningful life.

Along a somewhat similar vein in terms of ethics, Chapter Six looks to various texts that highlight ethical concerns. Melissa Ames's "Bodies of Debt: Interrogating the Costs of Technological Progress, Scientific Advancement, and Social Conquests through Dystopian Literature" is a pedagogy-focused chapter that discusses the successes and challenges of teaching a cross-curricular course on science and literature. The course studied narratives that wrestle with ethical concerns surrounding "progress" (societal achievements, technological and scientific discoveries, etc.). Some contemporary debates addressed in this course included: cloning, stem cell research, human trafficking, and capital punishment, and students analyzed various fictional texts (for example, Margaret Atwood's *The Handmaid's Tale* and Aldous Huxley's *Brave New World*, along with contemporary film companion texts such as *I, Robot* and *Repo Man)* that critique these issues. Class discussion revolved around the following questions: what do we do when human survival and societal progress come at extreme costs, and how might such advancements question our faith in humanity?

The Body in Popular Discourse

Section Two moves away from literary/filmic narratives and looks instead to popular culture to tease out actual spaces in which the body is highlighted and interrogated. In Chapter Seven, "Selling Weddings and Producing Brides: Mediated Portrayals of that 'Perfect Day,'" Sarah Himsel Burcon analyzes various mediated portrayals of American weddings in order to problematize marriage "performances" that are arguably grounded in materialist concerns. The essay points out how weddings, which were once small, private affairs, have now become a $48 billion industry, with the average cost of a U.S. wedding in 2012 being around $28,000. The essay takes a historical look at weddings, ultimately arguing that cultural products depicting weddings, such as magazines, films, and television shows, often work to reinforce the traditional status quo that connects women with domesticity, rather than to resist stereotypes by offering up stronger models of femininity.

Gender is also significant in Chapter Eight, Kristi McDuffie's "Epideictic Rhetoric in *Jezebel's* Breastfeeding Blogs: The Battle for Normalcy." This chapter examines breastfeeding rhetoric in recent years. Breastfeeding rhetoric, which has proliferated in recent public discourses about debates over breastfeeding, elicits some of the strongest praise and blame rhetoric in contemporary U.S. public discourses. One particular online women's blog, *Jezebel,* demonstrates the variation and strength of this rhetoric in its scope and tone of its posts. By looking at the praise and blame rhetoric, or what Aristotle calls epideictic rhetoric, of breastfeeding discourse in *Jezebel,* this chapter finds that breastfeeding rhetoric encompasses constant arguments for what should be normative about breastfeeding. Following Judy Segal's application of epideictic rhetoric to medical discourses and utilizing Lennard Davis's concept of normalcy, this chapter analyzes breastfeeding rhetoric as a site of contention about normalcy regarding women's bodies, behaviors, and values. Ultimately, this analysis determines that the use of epideictic rhetoric, as well as corresponding rhetoric that argues for any behavior to be normative in women's lives, is not supportive of women; instead, breastfeeding rhetoric should refrain from arguing for any particular norm and embrace diversity in women's bodies and women's lives.

The final chapter examines the ways in which prison literature might act to carve out an identity for Life Without Parole (LWOP) prisoners. Chapter Nine, "The Forever Indebted Body: Life Without Parole" by Adrienne Bliss, draws on prisoners' real-life accounts and examines how individuals who are sentenced to life without parole have to go through the process of learning how to live as less than or marginalized due to incarceration. The chapter points out that these prisoners must also reconcile with the fact that society will *never* let them return. Ultimately, it questions the cost to society, emotionally and economically, given the fact that the United States has an increasingly aging prison population and is also one of the very few nations that sentences juveniles to LWOP.

As a whole, these chapters work to both prompt and continue conversations surrounding the body, and specifically, bodies that can be labeled "indebted." *Fabricating the Body* brings together issues of gender, class, and identity, and investigates ethical concerns along with topics related to marginalization and the mind/body split. Finally, it problematizes issues related to Modernity and postmodern culture - such as disruption, contradiction, performance, and fragmentation - in order to position the body as a productive space for academic research.

SECTION I:

THE BODY IN LITERATURE

CHAPTER ONE

A PARATACTIC "MISSING LINK": DORIAN GRAY AND THE PERFORMANCE OF EMBODIED MODERNITY

RACHEL HERZL-BETZ

In 1883, at the infamous Westminster Aquarium[1], G.A. Farini introduced the newest addition to his freak show tour: a seven-year-old girl from "Indochina" who was professionally known as "Krao, the Missing Link" (Durbach, *Spectacle* 57). She would remain an integral part of the international freak show circuit for forty-five years, but her career began at the "Aq," where prostitutes prowled the promenade and where sea creatures were quite beside the point (Durbach 58). Krao's first audiences had the chance to judge her validity as a genuine missing link in Darwin's evolutionary chain. One such observer, from *The Continent,* emerged equally delighted and confused:

> It will be seen that her legs from the knee down and her arms from the elbow down are quite too long for a human child; yet in her great black lustrous eyes seems to shine an intelligence far above that of the brute creation. Her ability to speak, to learn even the ways of civilization, seem to warrant the belief that she ought to be ranked with the race which cooks and prints and laughs and talks. But what shall be inferred from the marks and features which seem to emphatically connect her with a lower order of beings? (240)

How, he wonders, can Krao exist as both the brute and the civilized human? Her body appears to fit the narrative Farini concocts about "a strange family of human monkeys" discovered in "Upper Birmah," but her mind does not match (240). The question appears throughout the coverage of Krao's late-Victorian tours. Another article glibly juxtaposes the

---

[1] See Durbach 57-58 for the Aquarium's history as venue for freak acts, variety shows, and prostitution.

supposed pouches in her mouth and the extra "dorsal vertebrae" in her spine with her "mild, affectionate, and remarkably intelligent" nature (*Michigan* 7). Krao appears to represent two identities simultaneously, a trait she shares with most late-Victorian freak show performers and which sets her apart from almost every performer outside of the Victorian context. Yet, few critics within freak studies have explored the significance of a gap between the freakish body and the freakish mind.[2]

This essay holds that the critical silence about the mind/body gap Krao shared with countless other "freaks" comes down to a problem of context. Critics have not counterposed late-Victorian freak show discourse with another performance of separated identity constructed near the Westminster Aquarium. During Krao's time in London, Oscar Wilde composed his only novel, *The Picture of Dorian Gray*. There, he tells the story of a man whose mind and body are split into separate entities as he performs a heightened version of himself for his friends and curious servants. At the urging of his mentor, Lord Henry Wotton, Dorian fashions his life as a performance of endless physical beauty, while his portrait symbolically enacts his mental degeneration behind closed doors. Critics commonly contextualize Dorian Gray and his decadent compatriots through an upper-class form of social Darwinism popularized by Max Nordau and Cesare Lombroso. In fact, social Darwinism and decadence have long existed as paired phenomena in the conversation surrounding late-Victorian literature. Critics variously associate H.G. Wells's Eloi, Robert Louis Stevenson's Hyde, and Bram Stoker's Dracula with the fear that humanity could return to pre-modern monstrosity. The freak show contributes to the discourse of, but has often been read as too pre or non-modern to comment on, the decadent man. As a result, critics have yet to contextualize Dorian's divided identity through non-normative performances taking place down the street from his artistic inception.

---

[2] Like others in freak studies, I refer to the performers I study as "freaks" and to their places of employment as "freak shows." My chosen language is not intended to signify an inherent non-normativity, nor do I seek to reify a spectacular relationship between the human object on stage and the, supposedly, normative observer. Instead, I refer to the performers by their job description because, when they are on stage and in character, they are performing as freaks. My choice of terminology is not meant to negate the victimization of many performers in the industry and should not be taken as a reflection on current performances of non-normativity. Members of the contemporary disability community are not "freaks" unless they choose to frame and perform themselves as, contextually, "enfreaked" (Thomson, *Freakery*). Disability and freak studies overlap, but they still represent separate fields with distinct foci.

I argue that juxtaposing the freak and the aesthete highlights their shared gap between body and mind. Both performers create fragmented identities, which other agents stage, frame, and control. Placing the freak show beside the decadent performance redefines each discourse and contradicts current critical dogma: first, the freak show's explicit perfomativity highlights the many agents framing Dorian Gray's aesthetic identity. Second, the aesthetic novel's emphasis on contradictions between embodiment and interiority highlights the juxtaposition of mind and body in each freak show performance. Using a theoretical framework proposed by Susan Stanford Friedman, I further claim that parataxis, "the juxtaposition of things without providing connectives" (494), best captures the disjunction and the creative potential of the freak performance. The performer's embodied parataxis places the freak show where it properly belongs: within ongoing debates about how to define the modern, if the modern is understood as a disruption and fragmentation of "conventional sequencing, causality, and perspective" (Friedman 494-95). Indeed, the late-Victorian freak performer embodies the fragmentation, discontinuity, and contradiction more commonly associated with aesthetic Modernity. I demonstrate this hitherto overlooked connection by viewing the late-Victorian freak show beside and through *The Picture of Dorian Gray*. This juxtaposition not only highlights a key historical context shaping Wilde's protagonist, but it also reveals a form of Modernity at the heart of every freakish performance.

Framing the Freak Show

Freak show discourse has been read as pre-modern or anti-modern in part because of its extensive history. Robert Bogdan, Rachel Adams, and other foundational scholars in the field now known as freak studies have established the freak show's continued success since the early modern era. Curious consumers could pay to see human anomalies in marketplaces, taverns, coffeehouses, and public fairs from the 1500s until well into the 20th century. Although "liminal" bodies maintained their appeal for more than 500 years, that appeal morphed from early modern wonder into 18th century curiosity. With the late 18th and early 19th century rise of statistics and eugenics, freak shows began to merge scientific and spectacular discourse, offering skeptical viewers the chance to test the unknown.[3] Only in the mid-19th century, with the establishment of abnormality as a

---

[3] For a history of the freak show and normalcy, see Rosemarie Garland Thomson and Lennard J. Davis.

coherent category, did performers become known as "freaks of nature" or simply "freaks" (Durbach, *Spectacle* xvi).

Between early performances of abnormality and their contemporary cousins, the freak show developed a series of recognizable structures and rhetorical moves meant to frame the spectacular body for public consumption.[4] Although, as Rachel Adams argues, "freakishness is a historically variable quality" shaped by temporally, geographically, and culturally specific definitions of deviance, "theatrical props, advertising, and performative fanfare" cued audiences to expect a freakish identity (5). Creating a heightened role for performers was always central to the freak show experience, but during the late 19th and early 20th centuries, top managers turned their shows into finely tuned machines. For those impresarios who initiated, supervised, and controlled popular acts, everything under their domain "framed and choreographed bodily difference" (Thomson, *Extraordinary* 71). The freak show's self-conscious framing process began before audience members stepped into the performance space and followed them when they left. Outside the tents or temporary "showshops," barkers echoed their own advertisements as they called to passersby, promising contradictory performances marked by their epigrammatic titles (Durbach, *Spectacle* xx). Figures such as the "Ugliest Women," the "Hottentot Venus," or the "Hairy Belle" created interest through surprising reversals in which one term "pervert[ed]" the second (Thomson, *Extraordinary* 71). Within the performance space, audience members turned towards the "elevated freak platform," where a costumed figure enacted repetitive choreography that reinforced the freak's fabricated history, while another barker walked through the audience spouting a constant stream of "blatant contradictions and inconsistencies" (Thomson, *Extraordinary* 60, Blyn, *Stage* 145). At the end of the show, audience members could purchase a staged image—or *"carte de visite"*— of their favorite performer encased in a literal frame (Bogdan). Shows that thrived during their late 19th and early 20th century heyday turned the problem of sideshow dishonesty into one of its greatest appeals.

A growing field of scholars argues that the middle classes used the freak show's conscious construction to shape England's developing Modernity, but upper and middle-class commentators tended to dismiss the freak show as a pre-modern response to a scientific problem. Show managers incorporated scientific curiosities as soon as they were published, but the rise of social Darwinism discredited that curiosity as

---

[4] For further discussion of the contemporary freak show, see Elizabeth Stephens and Eli Claire.

uneducated and vulgar (Thomson, *Extraordinary* 58). In 1859, at the closing of Bartholomew Fair, journalist Henry Morley spoke for his entire cultural community when he celebrated England's recovery from its collective "taste for Monsters" (246). The freak show had become so tightly tied to the past, that Morley conflated the end of one performance venue with the end of the genre, thereby ignoring five flourishing shows in nearby Whitechapel (Williams 6-11).[5]

Rather than turning to Tom Thumb or "Jo-Jo the Dog-Faced Boy" to confront questions of abnormality, Victorians increasingly turned to theories of atavistic science forwarded by Cesare Lombroso's *Criminal Man* and Max Nordau's *Degeneration*. Nordau argues that the decadent lifestyle of British and French aesthetes represents an evolutionary reversal, while Lombroso focuses on the degenerate criminal. Since the 19th century, critics have read both arguments as immensely influential for decadent authors. The popularity of such associations is, to an extent, justified. English translations made both texts widely available, and Nordau identifies Wilde as the chief "representative" of literary atavism (309, 317). At the same time, freak show impresarios created their own version of atavism, but scientific and literary communities refused to regard freak shows as contributors to an ongoing debate about the meaning of the atavistic body. On a basic level, every version of atavism originates in a misreading of Darwin's *Origin of Species* and builds from Ernest Haeckel's argument that individual development "recapitulates" the development of the species or, in other words, "ontogeny recapitulates phylogeny" (113). Following Darwin's demonstration that humanity has passed through a process of evolutionary stages, Haeckel argues that children re-enact evolution as they move through the developmental process; the individual essentially "climbs its own family tree" (Gould 114). Degeneration, in turn, can be defined by those cases in which development stops before the individual reaches evolutionary Modernity. Such individuals become "evolutionary throwbacks in our midst" or "atavists" (Gould 124). Lombroso, Nordau, and other upper-class Social Darwinists read physical atavism as the mark of an equally degenerate mind, and literary critics have ignored the alternate philosophy that freak shows created for their new audiences.

At the end of the 19th century, Victorian freak shows drew an increasingly working-class clientele, and that new audience was uncomfortable with the "tomfoolery, crowds, and class insubordination"

---

[5] For the relationship between the former site of Bartholomew Fair and the Whitechapel neighborhood, see *Cross's London Street Directory 1851*.

encouraged by the international freak show circuit (McHold 24). Even lower class audience members aspired to bourgeoisie morality, so the shows invented their own form of atavism, which contradicted Nordau and Lombroso's upper-class conflation of mental and physical degeneracy. Performances that had celebrated wild liminality began to emphasize a respect for the markers of middle-class identity, including "gender difference, domestic virtue, hard work, productivity, and consumerism" (Durbach 22). Impresarios juxtaposed the appeal of degeneration with middle-class morality by presenting their ugly women and wild children as mentally and spiritually civilized. Their bodies might remain abnormal, but their souls could be pure. Thus, when established characters came to England, their costumes, printed materials, illustrations, and origin stories shifted to reflect traditional marriage, families, leisure activities, acquisition, and labor. Female "oddities" asserted their interest in "feminine handiwork," married anew at each stage of a tour, displayed borrowed children, and performed dances dressed as Victorian children (McHold 28, Durbach 146). For Krao's first tour across the Atlantic, a local newspaper depicted a "neatly dressed Krao" beside a "decidedly more simian version of herself" copied from earlier pamphlets (Durbach, *Spectacle* 71). Readers of the *Peru Republic* could still see the large lips, hairy arms, and dark complexion that marked her degenerate body, but her new costume and demeanor indicated that a British soul had always waited within.

In spite of the freak show's active engagement with atavistic discourse, contemporary scholars have ignored how freakish performance is, itself, modern. Scholars studying 19th century freak shows from a disability studies perspective commonly claim that audiences used their presumed difference from non-normative spectacles to define themselves as culturally modern.[6] At the same time, a small number of literary critics point to early 20th century authors who used freakish discourse within literary modernism.[7] Together, they suggest that the freak show can only become part of Modernity or modernism through someone else's eyes. Either the Victorian audiences must use their interpretive power to transform the pre-modern into the modern or, as Robin Blyn suggests, modernist authors must use the freak show "as a formal strategy" to turn the "pitiful freak" into a "social renegade" (138, 146). In contrast, I argue that freakish discourse does not need a helping gaze to take part in modernity. Turning now to Wilde's *Dorian Gray,* we will see how

---

[6] For examples, see Rachel Adams and Rosemarie Garland Thomson.

[7] For two direct examples, see Robin Blyn's "From Stage to Page: Franz Kafka, Djuna Barnes, and Modernism's Freak Fictions" (2000) and "*Nightwood*'s Freak Dandies: Decadence in the 1930s" (2008).

Modernity and freakish performance function in mutual constitution in the Victorian period.

The Enfreakment of Dorian Gray

The greatest strength of a comparison between the late-Victorian freak show and Oscar Wilde's *The Picture of Dorian Gray* begins with the two discourses' obvious dissimilarities: the freak show exists to glorify useless ugliness, while decadent aestheticism celebrates useless beauty. The impresario's bearded women and giant men are, ostensibly, born to a life of freakish abnormality, while the aesthete crafts his own non-normative identity. Perhaps most damningly, aesthetes may choose to become unusual because they are economically independent. Unlike the freakish performer, who takes to the stage for sustenance, the aesthetic figure can afford to gild his home, his friends, and even his pets.[8] If the freak and the aesthete do not share an aesthetic appeal, a biological origin, or a sense of economic urgency, it seems fruitless to force such dissimilar discourses into a common space, where equivalencies come to little more than coincidence. However, the dissimilarities between freakish and decadent performances lend creative potential to their stark juxtaposition. The two late-Victorian methods of presenting non-normative bodies should not be reduced to variations on the same theme; responsible comparisons attend to the differences between mentally disabled men, women, and children who performed as "Aztec Wonders" and wealthy men who performed as young dandies for equally affluent friends (Bogdan 131). Such comparisons also attend to their common structural similarities, which only appear in light of more obvious difference. By paratactically aligning the two and resisting the impulse to make one discourse permanently subordinate, we can trace the commonalities that render freakish and decadent rhetoric dependent on one another.

Juxtaposing freak shows and *Dorian Gray*'s decadent performers reveals two central commonalities. First, the two discourses share a structure of distributed agency, in which many participants frame each performance. When Krao steps onto the freak platform, her impresario, barkers, visual representations, and audience construct her performance identity, just as Dorian's many handlers, images, and observers turn him into the embodiment of his age. Neither the freak nor the aesthete creates his or her performance in a vacuum, and their framing undermines

---

[8] See *Against Nature* for Des Esseintes's decision to "have his tortoise's buckler glazed with gold" (Huysmans 41).

attempts to think of either discourse as biologically determined. Second, freakish and decadent performances share a systemic division between the performer's external body and his or her moral, spiritual, and intellectual interiority. Gaps between *The Picture of Dorian Gray*'s narrative genres echo similar gaps between its protagonist's body and mind, as well as gaps between the freak's body and mind. Suddenly, the gaps demand our attention. They multiply upon one another, revealing the paradox at the heart of both performances: to draw a middle-class audience, freaks and aesthetes must maintain two irreconcilable identities. The two personas overlap, connect, and contradict, creating possibility through difference.

Counterposing the constructed, freakish world of Krao Farini with the aesthetic world proposed by Oscar Wilde highlights how many agents control Dorian Gray's non-normative performance. In Oscar Wilde's discursive freak show, Lord Henry Wotton, Dorian's dandified friend, declares himself Dorian's master of ceremonies. From the first, the good lord owns that "to a large extent the lad was his own creation" (Wilde 385, 409). Basil Hallward, who paints Dorian's infamous portrait, may be the first to order Dorian "up on the platform," but Lord Henry becomes Dorian's impresario, barker, and embodied advertisement in one (Wilde 386). Like a good manager, Lord Henry finds a naturally extraordinary figure and nurtures him into a performer. As Dorian stands upon the little stage, Henry shows him what power can come from abnormality and teaches him to love the "the hollowness, the sham," and the "silliness of the empty pageant" (Wilde 387, 425). Like a successful barker, Henry finds constant occasions for performances at dinners, "private views" "charity concerts," and the opera (Wilde 429). Like an educational pamphlet about a freak performer, Lord Henry equates his influence to conducting an "interesting study" for the good of "natural science," giving his work a veneer of moral respectability (Wilde 408). Calling attention to the ways that Lord Henry frames Dorian, Gray's aesthetic performance seems almost too obvious, but traditional readings have yet to combine Dorian's framers into a system of distributed agency.

The literal frame around Dorian's ageless portrait offers the most direct symbol of his many controlling agents. Like the frames around freak show illustrations, the border around Dorian's portrait defines the boundaries of an image, which, in turn, defines Dorian Gray. Others create it and try to sell it, while arguing that the image should be considered a more accurate representation of Dorian's identity than his physical presence. As long as Basil controls Dorian's portrait, he believes that he can claim a distillation of Dorian's identity. Freak shows offered a similar chance to capture a freak and take him/her home. As audience members left, shows sold framed images of their performers as mementos and, like Dorian's portrait, they offered the promise of capturing an unchangeable essence of the performer's identity. While the living performer changed and aged, the illustration promised to hold onto the performer's freakish essence; however, Dorian and the exhibited performers violated that promise: freaks often maintained the same performance identity over an entire career regardless of age, while their illustrations were adjusted to fit passing fads (Durbach, "Missing" 134). Like Dorian, their portraits aged and their bodies remained, on the surface, unchanged.

If the juxtaposition of the aesthete and the freak allows us to envision Dorian as a living exhibit, then who becomes his captive audience? Dorian performs for his peers, but his maids, footmen, and butlers provide a more fitting corollary for the freak show's middle-class audience. Traditional readings of *The Picture of Dorian Gray* imagine servants at the mercy of tyrannical aesthetes who monopolize the narrative's social and visual agency, but reading the aristocrat beside the freak reverses the power of the gaze and locates it in the servant, equating Dorian with the lowest social pariahs who exhibit their bodies to survive. The context of freak show discourse takes Dorian's paranoia about the horror of having "a spy in one's house" and of "rich men who had been blackmailed all their lives by some servant" and turns that fear into fact (Wilde 446). The accumulation of watching bodies suggests that his servants only wait for the best moment to use their secrets. Dorian's peers may joke about how they "daren't" punish their servants' misdeeds, but their humor hides a genuine fear of lower-class observation (Wilde 446). Like the freak show audience, the novel empowers butlers and maids to watch their employers and thus validate their own relative normalcy. For themselves and for their employers, butlers and maids represent what the narrator refers to as "[r]eality in the shape of a servant" (Wilde 400). Both aristocrats and the lower classes use one another to shape their respective identities, but freak show discourse gives the servants interpretive control. They watch and define the atavistic aesthete as the parasitic counterpart to their own laboring bodies. Rather than negating Dorian's agency, calling attention to Dorian's directors demonstrates how he exhibits himself within and against others' interests.

The Picture of Dorian Gray's divided form further establishes its status as a freakish textual performance. Since its publication, critics have identified two competing generic trends within its pages: that of the formless, French decadent novel and that of the traditional *Bildungsroman*. Reviewers have been unable to define this "curious hybrid" of a novel that seems unsure whether to be "a novel or a romance" and, instead, "partakes of both" (Clausson 341, 340). Rather than wade into Wilde's generic confusion, most critics pick a genre and argue for its ascendance, thus turning a pair of possible forms into a hierarchy or battle. After the publication of Wilde's text, *The Daily Chronicle* and *The St. James Gazette* mourned the novel's resemblance to the "leprous literature of the French Decadents," while, more recently, Isobel Murrey celebrated its resemblance to the traditional self-discovery narrative (Clausson 342, 344). Those who engage with the text's generic instability tend to read *Dorian Gray* as "a flawed work, riven by generic dissonances," but the novel's juxtaposition of French decadence and English commodity culture also makes it palatable for a middle class audience (Clausson 343).

Dorian's original readers may have had an easier time identifying the experimental half of the generic marriage because Wilde references a contemporary symbol of aesthetic form. Early in his education, Lord Henry gives his *protégé* a book that fills his mind with "metaphors as monstrous as orchids" (Wilde 447). The tome goes unnamed, but Wilde's contemporaries would have recognized the "novel without a plot, and with only one character" as *A Rebours* by M. Joris Karl Huysmans who, by 1891, was already commonly read as the public embodiment of the decadent age (Wilde 447).[9] Huysmans creates a textual representation of the decadent lifestyle, without plot, characterization, or interaction, and Dorian sees the novel's protagonist as "a kind of prefiguring type of himself" (Wilde 448). Following its appearance, the narrative transforms into a miniature *A Rebours,* disappearing down a rabbit hole of sensations and collections. However, active Dorian Gray can only channel the anemic Des Esseintes for twelve pages, at which point the plot returns and Dorian runs off to his own birthday. Such moments, when Wilde downplays aesthetic sensation and homosexual desire, suggest a kind of ideological retreat. They seem to hint at a bolder, more decadent version of *Dorian Gray* that Wilde does not allow himself to reveal, as though the novel's purely aesthetic passages represented Wilde's true intent.[10] However, a juxtaposition with freakish discourse supports an alternate reading.

---

[9] As early as 1883, Paul Bourget described how *A Rebours's* narrative "unity decays to make way for the independence of the page, where the page decays to make way for the independence of the word" (Denisoff 38).

[10] Nils Claussen argues that the textual rewriting that took place between the story's original serialization in 1890 and its publication as a novel in 1891 undermines the novel's subversive potential. In the intervening year, Wilde minimizes aspects of the novel attributable to queer sexualities and creates a heterosexual subplot. Claussen claims that the author's changes rendered the novel

The formal gap between the two genres allows the novel to find purchase with middle-class readers, much as the freaks' performative gaps allow their shows to find purchase with middle-class viewers. As Denisoff argues, the author "consciously took part in the cultural machinery that was nurturing a less daring form of decadence for the masses" (40). Wilde's identity, and the identity of decadence as a whole, establishes itself not on pure aesthetic bliss, but on the calculated juxtaposition of upper class excess and respectable, middle-class consumerism. Wilde's formal combination and contrast of contradictory forms echo similar relationships between Dorian and his servants, as well as those between the freak show performer and his audience. The novel's paradoxical combination of abnormality and normality simultaneously defines Wilde's decadent performer and the irreconcilable parts of *Dorian Gray*'s narrative form. Just as the successful freak show performer must draw on both moral and degenerate identities to capture an audience, Wilde needs both the decadent experimental form and the *Bildungsroman*, because neither appeals to the middle class on its own.

Modernizing the Missing Link

The last section of my argument demonstrates how 19th century freak shows drew Victorian audiences by adapting many of the same methods of juxtaposition that gave aesthetic novels their populist appeal. It seemed that middle and lower class viewers were not interested in the complete alterity popular in America and on the continent, so late-Victorian impresarios created a freakish performer who could represent both degeneration and moral integrity, thus allowing nervous audience members to imagine themselves within a coherent, middle-class identity. An implied collaboration between managers and audiences sounds suspiciously like one of the two ways of "modernizing" freak show rhetoric referenced earlier in my argument. Once again, freakish minds and bodies cannot take part in Modernity without an observer's help, but the freak show's implications do not end in what Matei Calinescu calls the "practical modernity of bourgeois civilization" (4). In addition to its role in economic Modernity, freakish discourse also belongs in ongoing debates about the definition(s) of the modern.

When managers and impresarios created an innocent freak, they also created a freak show performer who juxtaposed two identities in the same

---

incapable of making a potentially radical statement about subversion and degeneration (344).

embodied performance. Physically, a performer's body displayed the marks of degeneration, but his or her clothing, behavior, and publicity materials indicated a civilized mind and spirit. If Modernity is indeed a relationship with contradiction in which performing multiple, irreconcilable identities embodies the same disruption and fragmentation of "conventional sequencing, causality, and perspective" that characterizes parataxis, then freak shows do not exist outside the modern, but rather at its disjointed heart (Friedman 494-95). By bringing freak show discourse into the modern conversation, I am not interested in reifying a false boundary between middle-class and aesthetic Modernity, or suggesting, in Ivan Kreilkamp's words, that Victorian culture's value "must lie in the degree to which it anticipates later developments" (605). Instead, I want to ensure that the Kraos of freak discourse take their place in debates about what it means to be modern.

On its own, Victorian freak show discourse has long been associated with multiplicity, but its commonalities with *The Picture of Dorian Gray* illustrate that the freak's identities do not mix, blend, or overlap; instead, they co-exist in uneasy contradiction. For a similar relationship of paradox through juxtaposition, we might consider the epigrams that characterize Wilde's narrative. While reflecting on his role in Dorian's self-performance, Lord Henry Wotton considers the "separation of spirit from matter" and breathes "[s]oul and body, body and soul—how mysterious they were!" (Wilde 409). Critics have commonly taken the sentiment at face value and thus argued for the pervasive influence of upper-class social Darwinism.[11] However, counterposing *Dorian Gray* with freak show discourse suggests that the first portion of Henry's thoughts belong in the long list of epigrams that make up the novel's preface. Dorian's literal and figurative separation from himself builds a gap between the aesthetic body and soul until Henry's juxtaposition starts to read like an encapsulation of the novel's contradictions. Lord Henry's linguistic contradiction cannot be conflated with the freakish body, but bringing the two into conversation highlights the paradoxes embodied within the freak show's paratactic Modernity.

---

[11] Social Darwinism hinges on the belief that physical "brand-marks" accurately indicate mental and spiritual degeneration, such that moral laxity can be read through bodily deformity (Nordau 17). Critics tend to read Wotton's musings as a reflection on how Dorian's morality and his rotting portrait perform the direct link between "body" and "soul" (Wilde 209). For recent examples, see Claussen (2003) and Bristow's introduction to the 2007 Oxford edition of *The Picture of Dorian Gray*.

As an embodiment of paratactic Modernity, the freak performer contains a series of contradictions in each of his or her performances, including the contradiction between subject and object, between forms of temporality, and between means of defining identity. In his 2000 philosophical exploration of *Modernity and Subjectivity*, Harvie Ferguson could be speaking directly about Krao or Dorian Gray when he calls on Habermas to define the gap between subject and object (or mind and body) as Modernity's defining quality (5). Through the modern subjective lens, "Body is not subordinated to Soul, or Soul to Body." Instead, humanity's internal and external identity have been "subdivided and fragmented," to the point where each body, mind, and soul might as well exist within their own "autonomous realm[s] of meaningful experience" (Ferguson 2, 192). Freak show performances, like Ferguson's vision of Modernity, define themselves through the space between irreconcilable images of self. In her frilly dress, Krao embodies her freakishness as a separation between the object her audience perceives and the subject who performs from her own experience.

Beyond the division between self and other, interior and exterior, freak performers embody less explicit temporal paradoxes, as their shows move between contradictory methods of measuring time. The late-Victorian freakish performance moves in two temporal directions simultaneously: the performer's body seems to move backward in time, to humanity's evolutionary past and a never-ending childhood, while the performer's mind accelerates into the modern future, embodying the "oscillating consciousness of the old and the new" that Marshall Berman describes as inherent to modernism (Walker 3). Freak performances juxtapose the retrogressive temporality of degeneration with Modernity's implied progression. Current scholarship may have rejected linear definitions of Modernity, but its tropes signified forward motion to Krao's paying customers.

While those consumers oscillated between the old and the new, they also had to grapple with the contradiction between the freak as both a representative of a collective history and as an individual entity. Social Darwinists, managers, and audiences endowed freak show performers with multiple symbolic identities, each of which carried the weight of a long history. The freak signified the moral history of human evolution, of the English nation, and of economic class; his/her performances stood for the audience's history *en masse*. At the same time, the freak was an individual whose morality or degeneration, according to most social Darwinists, also represented individual sin. Calinescu defines that same contradiction as an oscillation between historical and personal temporalities. He argues that

Modernity should be seen as the "irreconcilable opposition between the
public/historical long *duree* (of the many versions of deep time)," which
would include deep evolutionary, national, and economic time, "and the
personal, subjective, imaginative *duree*, the private time created by the
unfolding of the 'self'" (Calinescu 5). Although the freak was freighted
with multiple public histories, the concept of "private time" seems even
more difficult to quantify. For the freak performer, private time could
signify individual self-expression through one's paratactic performance,
but it could just as easily signify the mark of individual sin. The gaps
between individual and public time, like the gaps between mental and
physical identities, multiply as quickly as we try to tie them down. The
freak show embodies a certain type of relational, paratactic Modernity and,
as such, cannot help but split into irreconcilable fragments.

    If the freak does, in fact, embody paratactic Modernity, then tracing the
significance of that Modernity matters as much as a linguistic definition,
especially when we consider the multiplicity of contradictory definitions
in the field .[12] Would a freakish Modernity resemble the accelerating,
progressive, "practical" Modernity of the middle-class Victorian audience
member? Or, will freakish Modernity—as highlighted by an "enfreaked"
Dorian Gray—come closer to decadent dispersal, alienation, and
disintegration, in which Modernity betrays "oceans of liquid matter, only
needing expansion to rend into fragments"? (Walker 12). While middle-
class, economic Modernity is all efficiency and coherent order, decadent
Modernity rends that order into a culture of "flux, dissolution and
collapse" (Kreilkamp 14). Although the freak show takes part in both
discourses, its paratactic performance is, most importantly, a Modernity of
possibility and potential. In the freak show, fragmentation and
juxtaposition do not signify the collapse of that which was once whole.
Each performer's separate mental, physical, and spiritual identities have
always been constructed and separate, so their combination only offers the
potential for unexpected new creation. Unexpected juxtapositions cause
unexpected connections, which, in turn, inspire the next day's show.
Where Des Esseintes's decadent Modernity slowly saps him of his
remaining vigor, the freak apparatus creates a remarkably generative take
on the modern. Even though its return to the evolutionary past would seem
to forestall forward motion, the freak's insistence on difference takes a
potential turn back and turns it into pure potential.

---

[12] For an explanation and refutation of Modernity's contradictions, see Friedman's
"Definitional Excursions: The Meanings of Modern/Modernity/Modernism"
(2001).

Works Cited

Adams, Rachel. *Sideshow USA: Freaks and the American Cultural Imagination.* Chicago: U of Chicago P, 2001. Print.

Blyn, Robin. "From Stage to Page: Franz Kafka, Djuna Barnes, and Modernism's Freak Fictions." *Narrative.* 8.2 (May 2000): 134-160. Print.

—. "Nightwood's Freak Dandies: Decadence in the 1930s." *Modernism/modernity.* 15.3 (September 2008): 503-526. Print.

Bogdan, Robert. *Freak Show: Presenting Human Oddities for Amusement and Profit.* Chicago: U of Chicago P, 1988. Print.

Bristow, Joseph. "Introduction" *The Picture of Dorian Gray* by Oscar Wilde. Oxford: Oxford UP, 2008. Print.

Calinescu, Matei. *Five Faces of Modernity: Modernism, Avant-garde, Decadent, Kitsch, Postmodernism.* Durham, NC: Duke UP, 1987. Print.

Chemers, Michael M. *Staging Stigma: A Critical Examination of the American Freak Show.* London, UK: Palgrave Macmillan, 2008. Print.

Claire, Eli. "Listening to the Freaks: A History of Circus Tents and Everyday Gawking" *Brittingham Visiting Scholar Lecture.* U of Wisconsin-Madison P. Oct. 10, 2012.

Clausson, Nils. "'Culture and Corruption': Paterian Self-Development versus Gothic Degeneration in Oscar Wilde's The Picture of Dorian Gray." *Papers on Language and Literature.* 39.4 (2003): 339-64. Print.

Darwin, Charles. *On the Origin of Species by Means of Natural Selection.* London: John Murray, 1859. Print.

Davis, Lennard J. *Enforcing Normalcy: Disability, Deafness, and the Body.* NY: Verso, 1995. Print.

Denisoff, Dennis. "Decadence and Aestheticism." *The Cambridge Companion to the Fin De Siecle.* Ed. Gail Marshall. Cambridge: Cambridge UP, 2007. 31-52. Print.

Durbach, Nadja. "The Missing Link and the Hairy Bell: Krao and the Victorian Discourses of Evolution, Imperialism, and Primitive Sexuality." *Victorian Freaks: The Social Context of Freakery in Britain.* Ed. Marlene Tromp. Columbus: The Ohio State UP, 2008. 134-154. Print.

—. *Spectacle of Deformity: Freak Shows and Modern British Culture.* Berkley: U of California P, 2010. Print.

Ferguson, Harvie. *Modernity and Subjectivity.* London: University Press of Virginia, 2000. Print.

Friedman, Susan Stanford. "Definitional Excursions: The Meanings of Modern/Modernity/Modernism." *Modernism/modernity*. 8.3 (Sept. 2001): 493-513. Print.

Gould, Stephen Jay. *The Mismeasure of Man*. New York: W.W. Norton & Company, 1981. Print.

Haeckel, Ernst. *The History of Creation Vol. II*. NY: D. Appleton and Company, 1887. Print.

Hale, David and the MAPCO. Cross, J. [pub.] *Cross's London Guide. Cross's London Street Directory 1851*. Accessed via Map and Plan Collection Online. http://mapco.net. Web.

Huysmans, Joris-Karl [trans] Robert Baldick. *Against Nature (A Rebours)*. London, UK: Penguin Classics, 2003. Print.

"Krao--a Missing Link." *The Continent; an Illustrated Weekly Magazine* (1883-1884), 5.106 (1884). Print.

"Krao." *Michigan Farmer* (1843-1908), 16.3 (1885): 1843-1908.

Kreilkamp, Ivan. "Victorian Poetry's Modernity." *Victorian Poetry*. 41.4 (Winter 2003): 603-611. Print.

Lombroso, Cesare. [Trans] Mary Gibson and Nicole Hahn Rafter. *Criminal Man*. Durham: Duke UP, 2006. Print.

McHold, Heather. "Even as You and I: Freak Shows and Lay Discourse on Spectacular Deformity." *Victorian Freaks: The Social Context of Freakery in Britain*. Ed. Marlene Tromp. Columbus: The Ohio State UP, 2008. 21-36. Print.

Morley, Henry. *Memoirs of Bartholomew Fair*. London, UK: Frederick Warne and Co. 1874. Print.

Nordau, Max. *Degeneration*. Lincoln: U of Nebraska P, 1993. Print.

Peru Republican, 24 April 1885, in Newspaper Advertisements, 1884-91. Circus World Museum, Baraboo, WI. Print.

Stephens, Elizabeth. "Twenty-First Century Freak Show: Recent Transformations in the Exhibition of Non-Normative Bodies." *Disability Studies Quarterly*. 25.3 (2005). Print.

Tromp, Marlene. "Introduction: Toward Situating the Victorian Freak." *Victorian Freaks: The Social Context of Freakery in Britain*. [ed] Marlene Tromp. Columbus: The Ohio State UP, 2008. Print.

Thomson, Rosemarie Garland. *Extraordinary Bodies: Figuring Physical Disability in American Literature and Culture*. New York: Columbia UP, 1997. Print.

—. "Foreword: Freakery Unfurled." *Victorian Freaks: The Social Context of Freakery in Britain*. Ed. Marlene Tromp. Columbus: The Ohio State UP, 2008. Ix-xi. Print.

Walker, Richard J. *Labyrinths of Deceit: Culture, Modernity and Identity in the Nineteenth Century.* Liverpool: Liverpool UP, 2005. Print.

Wilde, Oscar. "The Picture of Dorian Gray." *The Complete Works of Oscar Wilde.* New York: Dorset Press, 1995. Print.

Williams, Montagu. *Round London: Down East and Up West.* London: Macmillan and Co. 1894. Print.

CHAPTER TWO

A GENDER IN DEBT: LABOR AND THE FEMALE BODY IN *MR. WROE'S VIRGINS*

EMILY J. WORKMAN KELLER

When it comes to proverbial debt, every child is born, as accountants would say, "in the red." We are indebted to our parents for creating our bodies, and for nurturing and sustaining them until we reach an age when we can realistically take care of ourselves. In the early 19th century, the cultural landscape in England was changing, with a central shift toward the devaluation of women's labor, rendering women practically powerless in the marketplace and also in their personal relationships with men. As a result of this new cultural landscape, many women in 19th century England were forced to grapple with a new sense of identity while struggling to find the means by which to survive. Many found themselves indebted to a male benefactor, whether this benefactor was a father, a husband, or, as we see in Jane Rogers's novel, *Mr. Wroe's Virgins*, a religious prophet with questionable motives[1]. This paper seeks to explore the cultural landscape of Rogers's novel and the effects that this landscape had on the women who struggled to fend for themselves in a culture that did not value their labor. To that end, this paper juxtaposes both 19th century theoretical

---

[1] *Mr. Wroe's Virgins* is a novel about the historical figure John Wroe, who founded and served as a prophet to the Christian Israelite Church in Ashton-under-Lyne from 1822-1831. While serving as prophet, Wroe claimed that the Lord had instructed him to take seven of the community's virgins "for [his] comfort and succour" (Rogers 1). The members of the Christian Israelite community complied with Wroe's request, and these young women ended up running Wroe's large home. In Wroe's home, the women were burdened with a great deal of domestic labor. The story of these virgins is the focus of Rogers's novel, which relates the historical tale using four points of view, expressing the inner lives of these virgins while weaving an overall tale of feminine subjectivity.

discourses and contemporary discourses in an in-depth study of Rogers's Hannah, who is arguably representative of Rogers's ideal 19th century woman, and who struggles to keep herself alive through her own means.

In order to understand Hannah as an "ideal woman" in any capacity, it is necessary to define this concept as it is utilized and represented by Rogers. To this end, this analysis shall turn to Mary Wollstonecraft, who provided an exhaustive study of women's roles in society in her feminist manifesto, *Vindication of the Rights of Woman*. Since this manifesto was published in 1792, its perspective is contemporaneous with the events that take place in Rogers's novel. Furthermore, the values that Wollstonecraft lauds in her writing are echoed in Roger's character, Hannah, thus situating Hannah as an ideal woman as defined by Wollstonecraft's *Vindication*. Within her text, Wollstonecraft begins by demanding equal human rights for women, suggesting that women should not be confined physically or mentally. Instead of being subjected to confinement, Wollstonecraft posits, women should be allowed to develop talents and skills that will make them more marketable and useful in society. Furthermore, Wollstonecraft writes that women should have a desire to improve their community and a need for more freedoms than they currently enjoyed. Most importantly, Wollstonecraft maintains the need for women to be educated, so that they might find means by which to survive autonomously, outside the bonds of marriage. Wollstonecraft is ultimately practical, as she acknowledges the need for women to defer when necessary, thereby peaceably finding their niche in a community and becoming useful and productive members of society. All of these guidelines are essential to a study of Rogers's Hannah.

As stated above, the woman's role in the early 19th century marketplace was shifting drastically, and this shift is central to the development of Rogers's virgins, particularly Hannah, the most industrious and promising woman in the novel. Judith Lowder Newton, in her essay "Power and the Ideology of 'Women's Sphere'," observes that:

> with the development of industrialization, home production of many household items declined … [and] as men's work separated further from the home, new definitions and perceptions of work were further developed, definitions and perceptions which made married work in the home less *visible* as work than it had been before. (889, emphasis in original)

This "*invisible* work" led to the devaluation of domestic labor that is captured in an 1810 article in the *Edinburgh Review*, where it is observed that "the time of women is considered worth nothing at all" (Newton 890).

It is historically acknowledged that, "apart from domestic service, textiles, stitching, and washing there was little else open to women of any class in England" (Newton 889). Due to these financial limitations, women were obliged to consider their fathers, and eventually their husbands, as their financial means of survival, all the while experiencing a cultural indifference to their own labor in the home. Rogers's novel also explores the problems of women working in factories, but this concern falls into the periphery of the argument presented in this essay. For the purposes of this argument, the seemingly inescapable framework of indebtedness that women experienced in the domestic realm is the cultural scene in which Rogers's virgins toil.

Given the pervasive combination of factors at play in early 19th century England – industrialization and woman's new role as a domestic worker – it is not particularly surprising that Rogers chooses to focus so much of her narrative on the domestic labor performed by the virgins in her novel. In the essay "*Mr. Wroe's Virgins*: The 'other Victorians' and recent fiction," B. E. Maidment claims that the virgins are "Forced to manage a large and inappropriate house on inadequate resources," and further observes that "much of the novel details the burdens of women's household duties" (159). What Maidment asserts is evident in the text, given that several chapters are dedicated to the details of running John Wroe's household. One scene is particularly striking in its focus and its topic, however, and that is the washing day scene. As Maidment notes: "there is ... a strenuously extended account of wash day that graphically depicts the detail of women's work as a collective ordeal" (159). Interestingly enough, the ordeal of washing day is a topic that concerned authors who were contemporaneous with Jane Rogers's setting in *Mr. Wroe's Virgins* – particularly Anna Lætitia Barbauld – which renders this scene even more remarkable for an analysis of Rogers's depiction of England's cultural landscape.

Rogers tells the wash day story from Hannah's perspective, and Hannah describes the day as the ultimate trial, or "burden," for all the women, with them rising at the break of dawn to "scatter to [their] various tasks" (103). Although this task seems incredibly challenging, it is absolutely necessary that these women complete it. They must toil in order to earn their continued place in John Wroe's home. As women, their only hope is to please the prophet so that they can continue to be protected by him. The virgins (excluding Hannah) do not have skills that lie outside the domestic realm, so mastering these domestic tasks is their only hope of survival. Hannah's task is particularly arduous on this washing day, since she must "[draw] the twenty-eight buckets of water it takes to fill the copper" (Rogers 103). Hannah continues to relay every minute detail, from the "little anxieties" that occur to Joanna, their leader, to the "difficult business" of "opening and closing the tap," to the innovative approach that she herself develops in their method of retrieving hot water (Rogers 104). The tedious description found in this particular scene seems unremarkable at first glance, since many scenes in this novel focus on domestic duties. However, as Maidment's statement attests, this scene is noteworthy because of Hannah's in-depth explanation of each woman's duty and of their collective responsibilities regarding the task at hand, including Hannah's own role as the innovator. Hannah develops an improved method for filling the buckets with water that saves everyone time and effort, proving herself to be the most forward-thinking woman of the group. She also falls in line with the rest of the women and knows when to listen to their leader, Joanna. In this way, Hannah demonstrates some of the qualities that the ideal woman must possess in order to successfully navigate through the patriarchal system in which she is currently entrenched. Namely, she defers to authority when it is in her best interest, and she can also adapt new methods for completing tasks, thereby improving the lives of those around her.

In addition to being innovative and selectively subordinate, Hannah reveals another of her invaluable characteristics in the washing day scene, which is her ability to find satisfaction through her labor. She does this when she reflects on the day, recalling: "That first lungful of steam … the hollow stomach, aching back and shoulders, sore, raw-skinned knuckles; the pitch of physical exhaustion I reach…" (Rogers 104). The focus on Hannah's body here reminds the reader that this exhausted vessel is the tool through which Hannah experiences the world. Although she works herself to a seemingly dangerous point of fatigue, Hannah will not be able to work her way out of that body, or out of her situation. This is because Hannah's labor as a woman is not valuable to her culture. Only when Hannah finishes the sentence above does the reader understand how insidious the culture of domesticity has become for her. Her seeming contentedness, or at least her acceptance, can be detected in the following statement, "…the pitch of physical exhaustion I reach is almost pleasurable, for I become light and giddy. Complete happiness can then be found in taking a single bite of bread and cheese" (Rogers 104). Even when Hannah's "bodice is soaked from splashing and from sweat," she finds joy in simple pleasures (Rogers 105). The fact that she is satiated by such simple fare, bread and cheese, also aligns her with the wholesome qualities of the working class. Moreover, the fact that she finds pleasure on such a day suggests that she finds satisfaction and joy in her labor, and that she has the strength and personality she will need to manage in a Socialist community[2], which is one of the options Rogers leaves available to Hannah at the conclusion of the novel.

Given the extensive historical research that went into this novel, it comes as no surprise that Rogers presents her reader with a familiar literary trope from the early 19th century. Consequently, Rogers's washing day shares several characteristics with Anna Lætitia Barbauld's 1797 poem "Washing-Day." Barbauld's blank verse poem is a mock-epic, beginning with a classically-phrased – if not classically-themed – invocation to the Muse: "Come then, domestic Muse, / In slip-shod measure loosely prattling on ... Come, Muse; and sing the dreaded Washing-Day" (3-8). The tone of the poem is diminutive from the outset. By describing the Muse as "prattling on," the speaker appropriates and warps the epic tradition in order to undermine it. In the mock heroic tradition of Alexander Pope's *The Rape of the Lock*, and anticipating the likes of Felicia Hemans in her 1828 collection *Records of Women,* Barbauld calls upon these Muses "turned gossips" who have "lost / The buskined step" (1-2). From the opening lines, the reader can see that the poet is questioning the epic tradition, or the tradition of the men who came before her, and that she is taking on the domestic realm as her subject.

Like *Mr. Wroe's Virgins*, "Washing-Day" renders the act of doing laundry a miserable and arduous process for the women involved, despite the poem's satirical and mocking tone. The speaker of the poem addresses the women who are particularly vulnerable to the toils of doing laundry as follows: "Ye who beneath the yoke of wedlock bend, / With bowed soul, full well ye ken the day" (Barbauld 9-10). Here, it becomes clear that the women who have married are those who will suffer the most on washing day. In fact, calling marriage a "yoke" under which the married woman "bend[s]" aligns the married woman with an indentured servant, or even with livestock. Overall, its negative connotations implicate the unseen husband and the cultural structure from the outset of the poem. The speaker goes on to lament the "bowed soul" (Barbauld 10) that married women must feel on this taxing day, implying that the washing day does not simply tax the woman's body, but her very essence. It degrades her and leaves her somehow less capable than she was previously. Now, this poem has mocking undertones, but the fact remains that washing day is representative of far more than a day of the week in which the women of

---

[2] See Barbara Taylor's book, *Eve and the New Jerusalem: Socialism and Feminism in the Nineteenth Century,* which explores the largely forgotten "socialist-feminist ideal" that was once central to the Owenite movement championed by Robert Owen from 1825 to roughly 1835.

the house wash their linens. Instead, it becomes a sign of the "yoke" of domesticity that women must assume in order to live as wives in the homes of their husbands, much like the "yoke" that John Wroe's virgins bear in Rogers's novel.

The distinction Barbauld is making between the sexes becomes further solidified as her poem progresses in its lament of "all the petty miseries of life" or, in this case, the drudgeries of cleaning clothes and linens (28). As the speaker relates, "though the husband try" he cannot "kindle mirth / From cheer deficient," nor can the "unlucky guest" garner anything other than "stinted courtesy" (Barbauld 53-5, 56, 49). Certainly, the men in this poem look at the process as outsiders. They do not offer their services, and although their physical strength might come in handy, this process is considered women's work. Just like John Wroe's virgins, the women in this poem earn their living through the services they perform around the house. Furthermore, these services are taxing and Sisyphean in both texts, rendering them trivial because the result is so short-lived, despite how necessary the task is.

The speaker shifts in the last third of the poem, taking on a younger point of view with the lines "I well remember, when a child, the awe / This day struck into me ... for then the maids, / I scarce knew why, looked cross, and drove me from them" (Barbauld 58-60). As a child, the speaker is aware of the distress, yet just like the men in the poem, she stands on the outside looking in on the process. Furthermore, the domestic laborers, or maids, are brought into the poem here. This is the first time that the poem acknowledges the hardships that the hired laborers suffered in this domestic task, and they do struggle, experiencing the same hardship as the speaker's mother, ignoring "their petted one" and earning their hard-won living through their arduous labor (Barbauld 64). These women are the unlucky females who have not married, and we see them earning a living within the confines of a patriarchal culture where their labor is not valued. The only woman who is excused from this task – besides the speaker, who is a young child – is the grandmother, the "eldest of forms [who] tend[s] the little ones" (Barbauld 68-69). In this way, the speaker relays the inevitability of washing day, where only the very young and very old are excused. This labor, requiring much bodily strength, exemplifies the larger issues faced by women in this society. The women toil, and despite their efforts, their labor is ultimately as unsung as it is unending.

The disdain toward washing day labor that is apparent in both Rogers's narrative description and Barbauld's poem complicates Hannah's role as a woman in the early period of industrialization. Unlike the speaker of Barbauld's poem, Hannah spends considerable time wondering about her role in society. Indeed, she is encouraged in her musings by none other than John Wroe. Although Hannah might possess a number of attributes that position her as a strong woman, her own view of the potential freedom that her strength and independence may afford her complicates a simple prescription for an ideal post-industrial feminist role. Thus, a closer look at the contemporaneous views on the roles women ought to play in society leads to a greater understanding of how Hannah's characterization functions in the text. Furthermore, it demonstrates how Rogers positions Hannah in relation to the patriarchal, post-industrial, early 19th century society.

Since the psychological effects of being a woman during this time have yet to be examined here, this analysis will now turn to Mary Wollstonecraft, as her *Vindication*, published in 1792, is a contemporaneous text that has much to offer. In Wollstonecraft's *Vindication*, she claims that a typical 19th century woman was necessarily dependent upon a man for support, but Wollstonecraft maintains that this "dependence is [only] *called* natural" (128, emphasis added). By calling into question the true nature of dependence, Wollstonecraft suggests that women should be freed from this yoke and educated so that they might choose to live more useful and autonomous lives. The freedom that Wollstonecraft calls for leads to more ambitious goals, and, as Barbara Taylor explains in her book *Eve and the New Jerusalem,* Wollstonecraft ultimately desires the "social and political liberation of 'the people' as a whole" (5). The goals of education and social liberation are also dominant topics under consideration in Rogers's novel, as one can see in the character of Hannah. In her *Vindication*, Wollstonecraft also reflects on the limited means by which a woman might support herself when she bemoans: "How women are to exist in that state where there is neither to be marrying nor giving in marriage, we are not told" (118). In Rogers's text, Hannah is the woman who has rejected marriage. Here, Rogers explores the options that were available to single women in the early 19th century.

Unlike the other virgins in the tale, Hannah has *chosen* the life of a single woman, an unusual choice that led to her life as a virgin in John Wroe's household. Furthermore, she is educated and is invested in making positive social changes in her community, two attributes that hold the utmost value for early feminists like Wollstonecraft. Most importantly, Hannah is the only woman in the text who might feasibly support herself, as she earns a small salary for her reading instruction. Maidment claims that "Rogers acknowledges the limited public space available to Victorian working women, but has nonetheless succeeded in finding a combination of factors – rational and progressive communitarianism, nascent trade unionism, working-class education – which offer a plausible or even heroic locale for Hannah's self-seeking" (164). Through Hannah, Rogers suggests that it was feasible for women to carve out a life within the confines of patriarchy, although the options for work were quite limited and financial security was difficult to achieve. However, the role that Hannah plays is far more complex because of Rogers's carefully nuanced representation of the cultural landscape Hannah must navigate.

Hannah has a very unusual and revealing relationship with John Wroe, and this largely stems from his "recognition of her power to choose," even if this power of choice is intimidating for her (Maidment 163). In fact, Hannah struggles with the same worries that Wollstonecraft relays in her *Vindication*, particularly when Wollstonecraft ponders how women can make a living outside the bonds of matrimony. Since Hannah has chosen not to marry, at least for the time being, she must navigate her society outside of these protective bonds, and with no female predecessors that she might look to for a model. When considering her options for the future, Hannah constructs a metaphorical situation, wherein she is a passenger in a small boat, in order to be able to conceive of her body's place in relation to the world. Here, the reader might be reminded of a theory put forth by Simone de Beauvoir, author of *The Second Sex*: "The body is not a thing, it is a situation: it is our grasp on the world and our sketch of our project" (65). Hannah's body determines her grasp on the world, and a close examination of Hannah's musings renders Maidment's claim, that "patriarchal oppression might nonetheless operate as a source of self-definition for women," readily apparent in Rogers's text (163).

Hannah begins her musing with the arguably over-confident interjection, "I am free!" (Rogers 144). This reminds the reader of an earlier comment she makes when she is considering her place in John Wroe's household, when she claims that "the very freedom from choice is an attraction" (Rogers 88). Here, Hannah is not free as the 21st century reader would conceive of freedom; rather, she is free from choice. Hannah goes on to relay a situation where she is placed in opposition to nature, which begs the reader to ask: is Wollstonecraft's question regarding the "natural" quality of "dependence" at play here (Wollstonecraft 128)? According to Hannah, as a woman she is a "tiny boat" being "borne along" on a "huge and lazy river" (Rogers 144). Hannah regards herself as insignificant and small in relation to the huge context of life, or post-industrial, patriarchal culture. Furthermore, since the "huge" river is in control of the boat, Hannah does not see herself exacting any control over her own life. Instead, she sees her life as managed by the impersonal force of nature. Interestingly, Hannah aligns her womanhood to a manmade craft and society to nature, thereby situating herself outside of nature and solidifying the pervasive quality of the patriarchal society that controls her "tiny boat." It is also notable that, just moments after claiming her freedom, Hannah admits that she is anything but free by discussing the powerful force of the current that controls her. This suggests that she is aligning herself with her earlier definition of freedom, which is a freedom *from* choice. Hannah goes on with a statement that complicates this definition with the words "I *think* I may determine my course" (Rogers 144; emphasis in original). She thinks she may determine her course, and John Wroe reinforces this idea, but *is* she determining her course? Furthermore, does she truly desire complete control over her course, or does she desire a different type of freedom?

What follows in Hannah's imagination is an attempt to gain a sense of autonomy, and to take control over her metaphorical boat. However, instead of wielding the tools she possesses with strength and determination, she "make[s] a little splashing" with her oar which descends into a "frenzy of dabbling" (Rogers 144). The reader might easily dismiss these efforts as half-hearted, but there are other possibilities for the inefficacy of Hannah's rowing capacity. Perhaps she has never seen this tool in action before. After all, Hannah has probably never seen a woman control her own destiny. This act of autonomy serves as a good start as far as contemporary readers might view it, as at least she is doing something to counter the power of the current. Despite the lack of skill Hannah demonstrates, her efforts garner results, when her boat responds with a "spin" and an eventual "sharp veer" (Rogers 144). The following sentence reminds the reader of the power of patriarchy, though, as the "gentle" yet powerful current "inexorably," or relentlessly, removes any sense of control that the boat may have developed (Rogers 144). This "frenzied," "dabbling" effort is thwarted by a "gentle" and "gradual" current (Rogers 144), highlighting the pervasive power of the river, and reminding the reader how much energy and guile it will take for Hannah to gain even a minimal amount of control.

With her next assertion, Hannah claims with conviction, "I *shall* put ashore" (Rogers 144, emphasis in original). This defiant tone runs contrary to her previous assertions, and it serves as a strong provocation, especially when she follows with, "I shall exercise my single right to land" (144). As Wollstonecraft states: "Gentleness, docility, and a spaniel-like affection are … consistently recommended as the cardinal virtues of the [female] sex" (118). In a world such as this, imagine the conviction Hannah must possess to be able to assert her own dominance with such determination. Hannah is rejecting the culturally defined virtues of her sex and defining

her own, claiming her "single right" to steer her boat ashore. The use of
the word "single" in this sentence begs closer inspection. Hannah may be
suggesting a freedom that she might enjoy as a single, or unmarried,
woman. On the other hand, she may be setting herself apart from her
female peers and suggesting she is the only woman in the text who has the
right to land. Perhaps she is suggesting both at once, and utilizing a double
entendre that allows the reader to decide Hannah's true character. In any
case, the fact remains that, in a time when women had no rights, Hannah is
carving out a small portion of autonomy for herself.

Unfortunately, it is not nearly so simple to change the current of
patriarchy, and for all the value inherent in Hannah's claims, she still
inhabits a female body, which simply holds no claim to power. After her
determination to "put ashore," Hannah is forced to admit that "the strength
of the current, the shape of the river, [and] the effects of the weather" will
also determine her course (Rogers 144). Nature lies outside the realm of
human control, but Hannah's relinquishment of power becomes
problematic when she mentions the "state of [her] vessel" (Rogers 144).
The vessel must refer to her body, and, if this is the case, Hannah is giving
up because she views her body as ill equipped to handle the task of self-
sufficiency. Here, a female cannot possibly row her way out of the current
of patriarchy and navigate the unknown shore of financial and
psychological autonomy, especially when these difficulties are coupled
with "a hundred factors perhaps beyond [her] control" (Rogers 144).
These factors have the power to thwart any endeavor Hannah might make
to crawl out of her inevitable indebtedness. It is significant that Hannah
still calls this unwillingness to land a "choice" at this point in the passage
(Rogers 144), for the reader has no option but to question whether Hannah
really is free to choose, despite her earlier claim. In fact, her conception of
freedom becomes clear here, as she most certainly desires a freedom from
choice, rather than the freedom to make choices.

Hannah's conception of freedom is further clarified when she admits
what the reader has sensed all along, that she ultimately believes "It would
be worse than anything to land, and stranded on the bank, regretting that
lost and hidden country just beyond the river's next lazy loop" (Rogers
144). After all the claims made regarding a desire to escape the current of
patriarchy, Hannah, the smartest and strongest of Wroe's virgins, simply
lacks the desire to escape her situation. Wollstonecraft writes of this very
phenomenon, claiming that women are "Taught from their infancy that
beauty is woman's scepter, the mind shapes itself to the body, and roaming
round its gilt cage, only seeks to adore this prison" (131). Like a victim of
Stockholm Syndrome, Hannah "roam[s] round [her] gilt cage ... ador[ing]

[her] prison," a female weakened by the patriarchy, and ultimately too frightened to even attempt an escape. Hannah continues in this vein with the claim that the "benefits" she "enjoys" within John Wroe's house "are the result of lack of liberty and equality" (Rogers 144). When a 21st century society looks back at Rogers's character, it is with a conflicting sense of shame, pity, and frustration. Admittedly, Hannah would have had extremely limited options available to her, but it excites the reader's sense of justice to see her acquiesce to the need for creature comforts when her liberty and equality are at stake. As she herself admits in the passage's conclusion, "I willingly live under the sway of a tyrant, and am grateful for that irresponsibility" (Rogers 144). Here, Hannah echoes her previous claim that "the very freedom from choice is an attraction" (Rogers 88), representing the mind trapped in a "gilt cage" (Wollstonecraft 131), and the reader wonders whether she will truly remain on the tiny boat to see what the next "lazy loop" will bring (Rogers 144).

It seems simple enough to consider Hannah's characterization as a straightforward struggle between individual rights and creature comforts. However, Rogers's character is far more complex than it might seem based on the river scene. As Maidment writes, "*Mr. Wroe's Virgins* seems to me a book that combines proper outrage at the lives under patriarchy with an equally proper awareness of the complexity of Victorian sexual politics" (165). An accurate understanding of the phrase "sexual politics" in this context will be a broad one, especially if it takes the role that Hannah plays in this novel into account. When Hannah explains her boat scenario, the reader is well aware of her past, in which she attended Owenite meetings and political lectures with Edward, a man who proposed marriage to Hannah and whom Hannah rejected. Hannah's relationship with marriage is not simple, perhaps because it is informed by the Owenite principles with which she is familiar. The Owenites were cautiously speculative about the reforms in divorce that were contemporaneous with the setting of Rogers's text. Despite their call for free love, the Owenite feminists did not necessarily want divorce; rather, they wanted happier marriages with laws to "enforce" the "obligations of marriage" rather than "abolishing" them (Taylor 205).

Rogers gives Hannah the opportunity to speak about the issue of marriage in her narrative. When Hannah tells Joanna of her past relationship with Edward, who had since "gone to America to live in one of Mr. Owen's new communities, founded upon principles of freedom and rationality," she is faced with Joanna's questions regarding the Owenite religion (Rogers 84). When Joanna asks, "Are not the Owenites against marriage?" she echoes the commonly held view of that religion. Hannah balks at this, complaining in an interior monologue: "Why is it that the most salacious rumours about a system of beliefs travel like wildfire, while its sober truths … are ignored?" (Rogers 84). Hannah replies with a great deal of patience and knowledge, explaining, "Some of Mr. Owen's followers have spoken out against marriage, as an institution which imprisons and degrades both parties, and which – in law – reduces the woman to no more than her husband's property" (Rogers 84). According to Hannah, the Owenites have ideas that will "confer upon humanity" some "great benefits" (Rogers 84). One of these is the religion's views on marriage, which are not as polarizing as Joanna implies, but instead promote more equitable roles. As Hannah asks in the conversation with Joanna, "What virtue can there be in love that is not freely exchanged, between equals?" (Rogers 84). This statement embodies the Owenite tradition, and it also encapsulates Hannah's own feelings on marriage quite accurately.

Given her views on marriage, it is noteworthy that Hannah turned down an offer of marriage to an Owenite man. After all, Edward, Hannah's would-be fiancé who later develops an aversion to the institution of marriage, writes of shared quarters for married couples as a means to engender "legalized prostitution enforced by marriage" (Rogers 140). Further, Edward describes the marriages he sees in America thusly: "Within families the relations between men and women are always those of possessors and possessed: the husband owns not only his wife but also his daughters, and seems to feel he has the right to decide upon their disposal, with complete disregard for their own wishes" (Rogers 139). Clearly, Edward, the man who declared to Hannah, "all my free thoughts are of you" (Rogers 141), would be an ideal match for a woman who wants a union where she is respected and loved. Instead, as Hannah herself states, she "willingly live[s] under the sway of a tyrant, and [is] grateful for that irresponsibility" (Rogers 144). Does Rogers really want her readers to believe that Hannah could be so weak, or is there more at stake here?

Hannah does not simply live in Mr. Wroe's household and consider her housework the only thing she will contribute to society. She attends lectures, such as the one held by William Cobbett, who "describe[s] the plight of the urban poor" and calls "the manufacturing process … one of the chief causes of the ills of society" (Rogers 147). Further, she teaches night-school classes for the Ashton and Stalybridge District Cooperative Society, in the hopes that literacy will improve the lives of factory workers (Rogers 148). In her own words to John Wroe, "Teaching [factory workers] to read … opens a door on to the world" (Rogers 197). Hannah's view of education is idealistic, and she feels as though she is improving the lot of her fellow men by helping them develop literacy skills. Hannah is also the only one of John Wroe's virgins who earns her own money, viewing the small sums she earns as "a start towards independence" (Rogers 154). Here, Hannah represents Wollstonecraft's ideal woman. She is educated, she is invested in improving her community, and she has discovered a means by which she might survive outside of marriage. This may be why Hannah chooses not to marry Edward, as the single life may be a necessary characteristic of the woman who can bring about social change.

This essay has revealed Hannah as a woman who chooses the single life, who teaches community members to read, who innovates the means by which her fellow virgins complete their arduous domestic tasks, and who sees herself as the willing participant in a flawed patriarchal system of subordination. Her female body has placed her in debt, and there are also limited means by which she might make a living. Further, she is fully entrenched in the idealistic notions of the early 19th century. Through Hannah, Rogers offers qualities that the ideal woman would have needed to possess in order to foster women's growth and move them toward the next stage of independence. Furthermore, Rogers uses Hannah as a means by which her readers might recognize the flaws in this society, particularly regarding industry and gender equality. Because Rogers has the advantageous vantage point of an historian, she can see the life options available to Hannah. However, instead of using this position to fix the problems of the past (which, of course, one cannot do), Rogers has chosen to illuminate them for her reader. In the end, there is no quick fix for the Hannahs of the world; they must plunge their way into the future and find a route toward equality. Certainly, Hannah is the ideal woman for the job, but Rogers's 21st century audience knows that even the ideal woman's road will be wrought with innumerable obstacles.

Works Cited

Barbauld, Anna Lætitia. "Washing-Day." *The Norton Anthology of English Literature: The Romantic Period*. Eds. Jack Stillinger and Deidre Shauna Lynch. New York: W.W. Norton & Company, 2006. 178-9. Print.

De Beauvoir, Simone. *The Second Sex*. London: Jonathan Cape, 1953. Print.

Maidment, B.E., *"Mr. Wroe's Virgins*: The 'other Victorians' and recent fiction." *British Fiction of the 1900s*. Ed. Nick Bentley. New York: Routledge, 2005. 153-66. Print.

Newton, Judith Lowder. "Power and the Ideology of 'Woman's Sphere'." *Feminisms: An Anthology of Literary Theory and Criticism*. Eds. Robyn R. Warhol and Diane Price Herndl. New Brunswick, NJ: Rutgers UP, 1997. 880-95. Print.

Rogers, Jane. *Mr Wroe's Virgins*. New York: First Mariner Books, 2000. Print.

Taylor, Barbara. *Eve and the New Jerusalem: Socialism and Feminism in the Nineteenth Century*. 1983. Boston: Harvard UP, 1993. Print.

Wollstonecraft, Mary. *Vindication of the Rights of Woman*. 1792. New York: Viking, 1985. Print.

CHAPTER THREE

THE COSTS OF DEBT:
THE INDEBTEDNESS OF THE FEMALE BODY
IN ARTHUR SCHNITZLER'S *FRÄULEIN ELSE*

MATTHEW J. SHERMAN

Arthur Schnitzler's *Fräulein Else* is saturated with contradiction and dissonance that hinge upon the position of the female psychological subject in relation to the social order. Entering the social order establishes the indebtedness of the psychological subject to the prescriptions of that order. This subject becomes entangled in conflict when personal desires are antithetical to social standards. In Schnitzler's novella, the primary conflict of the protagonist, Else, circumscribes her sexuality and the exposure of her body. Else's parents ask her to request 50 thousand gulden from a family acquaintance, Herr von Dorsday, who is willing to pay the sum if Else poses nude for him. The coinciding requests of her parents and Herr von Dorsday trigger conflict between her obligations to self and society, because she is bound to forms of indebtedness that are fundamentally oppositional. The thought of exposing her body creates psychical tension between her repressed sexuality and the internalized social and familial bonds. This paper appropriates a psychoanalytic framework to uncover the reciprocity of external and internal realities, to underscore the indebtedness of the female body to masculine desires in *fin-de-siècle* Vienna, and to locate *Fräulein Else* as a fictive paragon within this composite. Else's body is a social currency, void of autonomous signification, and imbued with irreconcilable conflict. She is trapped within a patriarchal structure, which limits female identity and prevents the reappropriation of the female body or female sexuality. Her only avenue to break the indebtedness of her body to masculine demands is to sever the social bond and take her own life.

Arthur Schnitzler's novella, *Fräulein Else,* is the inner monologue of a 19 year-old Viennese woman. Else is on holiday when she receives word from her mother that her father faces imprisonment, as he has once again accrued a large debt the family cannot pay. To maintain the family's livelihood and save her father, her mother asks Else to request the sum from a man who has helped them in a similar situation in the past: Herr von Dorsday. Dorsday agrees to pay the sum, but in return, he wishes to see Else nude. She contemplates the deed, her thoughts oscillating between repulsion and excitement. Else fantasizes about sexual expression and, specifically, the act of exhibition. In the end, she exposes herself in the music room of the hotel to many of the guests, including Dorsday. After fainting and being taken to her room, she takes a lethal dose of the sleep aid, Veronal.

The Debt of/to the Family

It is the literal debt of the father that exacerbates Else's conflict. His debt of 50 thousand gulden threatens not only his, but also the family's, livelihood and reputation. Else considers the repercussions of not paying the debt, the subsequent shame in the loss of social status, and the need to request the sum from Herr von Dorsday. Her obligation to carry out the parental request is thus bound up in the overlapping and reciprocal nature of the public and private spheres, a complex interconnectedness of the individual and society. For Else, this problematic relationship vis-à-vis her father's debt hinges upon the family's social status and her socially defined role as female. As a young unmarried woman, she is dependent on the financial support of her father, who has provided the bourgeois lifestyle to which she has grown accustomed. Her status and livelihood are bound to those of the family, specifically the patriarch.

Yet, the father does not play an active role in the novella. Rather, it is Else's mother who writes to inform her of the father's debt and to request that she ask Dorsday for the sum. The intent of the letters from the mother is vague, and its subtlety, a necessity of bourgeois sensibilities, demands deductive interpretation. It is neither coincidental nor inconsequential that it is her mother who asks on behalf of her father. This is unequivocally so that the mother may steer Else towards the allocated modes of payment within the patriarchal structure: "So I beg you, my dear girl, talk to Dorsday. I assure you there's nothing to it" (Schnitzler 200). This need to offer assurance suggests there is, in fact, something more to it. It also suggests that her mother has an understanding of how women can appeal to the inclinations of men. Her assurance implies a first-hand knowledge of appealing to a man for aid, as well as the simplicity of its success. This assurance, then, seems to locate the space of feminine persuasion. If this knowledge marks the domains of gender roles, then it is the mother who would educate Else on the domain of the feminine in relation to that of the masculine. Most importantly, however, the desire for Else's role in such persuasion begins to define her social and familial roles, and, therefore, the parental expectations of Else and their anticipation of Dorsday's subsequent request.

Else's mother's intentions are elucidated in her acknowledgment of Dorsday's affections for Else: "He's always been especially fond of you," she writes, at which point Else thinks, "– I never noticed that. True, he stroked my cheeks when I was twelve or thirteen: 'Becoming quite a young lady, aren't we?'" (Schnitzler 200). Her mother is intuitively aware of this physical "fondness," yet her request falls in line with the language of propriety. Else's unawareness as a child, but recollection as a young women, indicates that this fondness actually speaks to sexual interest. Therefore, Else would not have noticed Dorsday's interest, whereas her mother did. The implicit nature of the letter is exposed further through Else's responses while reading, which impugn the objective of her mother's words. These hostile doubts include, "Do you really believe that, Mama?" (Schnitzler 200-201). Else's sporadic, dismissive commentary indicates not only that she questions her mother's assertions, but also that she is suspicious of her mother's turn to Else as a last resort. It becomes clearer that Else serves a particular function when she questions, "Why didn't Papa just board a train and come here? – He would have arrived just as fast as the express letter" (201). In acknowledging that the rational option was not attempted, she rejects the fact that she was a last resort, and if she is not, then her approaching Dorsday stands as the preferred option for reasons that are not directly elucidated. Her suspicions regarding the intentions of her parents are made more apparent later in the novella:

> He must have guessed that Herr Dorsday wouldn't do it for nothing – otherwise he would have telegraphed or come here himself but it's easier and more convenient this way, isn't it, Papa? When one has such a pretty daughter, why should one have to march off to prison? And Mama, stupid as always, just sits right down and writes the letter. Papa didn't dare. If he had written it, I would have known it immediately. (Schnitzler 224)

Although she wavers on this assessment, it is the father who articulates the demand that Else pay her familial debt. The request of the father is cloaked in the request of the mother, who also seeks to sell their daughter to Dorsday. To do so, they take advantage of their "pretty daughter," whose sex appeal can secure their financial interests. Although Else acknowledges her mother's involvement, she ultimately places responsibility for the request upon the patriarch of the family, who exploits his daughter's sexual appeal to avoid being sent to prison. Else's mother is complicit in this exploitation. Because she is the wife of the patriarch, her livelihood and reputation are also at stake.

Else's Conflict

Dorsday's proposition for the exhibition of Else's nude body as compensation for the payment of the father's debt triggers the deterioration of her well-being, as it encompasses opposing obligations to family, society, and self. Her psychical conflict now reaches its apex. A psychoanalytic approach caters to the explorations of such conflict, not only in dealing exclusively with inner realities, but also the ways in which the social order constitutes this psychological turmoil. There is indefinite conflict within the psychical apparatus, which exists in the ego's attempt to satisfy not only external demands, but also those of the super ego and the id (Freud 17). I seek to present Else's sexual identity as inherently split, with her primary identification as antithetical to the desires/demands of the patrilineal social order. On one hand is her obligation to the desires of the id, specifically in the satisfaction of sexual desires. On the other hand is her obligation to the super ego, which contains both the internalized social and familial structures, including the learned influence of the parental figures (Freud 15-16).

The vacillations between her id and super ego are evident in both the flux of thoughts and the dissonance between thoughts and action. For example, when Else returns from a game of tennis she is asked "Back from tennis?" She thinks, *"Well it's obvious. Why does she ask?"* yet she responds, "Yes, madam. We played almost three hours" (194). This demonstrates a simple sense of social propriety, in which subjective thoughts are repressed or filtered into socially acceptable content. To some extent, this is a superficial example of the everyday use of filtering true thoughts to emphasize the petty nature of Else's bourgeois class. Yet, this shows that Else is consumed by the restrictions of her super ego, and emphasizes her inability to act against the social order in a relatively insignificant instance. Towards the opposite end of this spectrum is the sensitive domain of sexuality. Schnitzler illustrates this dissonance in a more dramatic and meaningful fashion by exposing Else's thoughts on her body and sexuality, a trope that enunciates the fissure between the public and the private, and thus underscores a fundamental conflict of the bourgeois female subject. The inner-monologue exposes this latent content in the exposition of actual dream content and preconscious thought, which provides access to these conflicts, and illuminates Else's indebtedness.

Else's thoughts and dreams regarding her subjective, id-based desires apropos sexuality are voluminous and exaggerated. One of her primary fantasies is to give her body to multiple partners. When she considers her sexuality and Dorsday's particular request, she adopts hyperbole, imagining that she might have "ten lovers, twenty, a hundred," exposing herself to as many people as possible (Schnitzler 232). While recalling her act of exhibitionism on a balcony in Gmunden, when she pretended not to notice two men watching her from a boat off in the distance, she thinks, "Yes, I'm like that, I'm like that. I'm a slut" (Schnitzler 223). In identifying herself as a "slut," the signification of her language operates within the symbolic order of patriarchy, yet this declaration, a confession of sorts, is a way of keeping her sexuality at bay. It is a simultaneous rejection of the sinner/saint dichotomy. She denies her gendered class identity as the "lady" who adheres to the image of feminine propriety produced in textual materials, like books on conduct, that provided the images of this refined lady (Skeggs 99). The form of her declaration, her word choice, symbolically speaks to the prohibited female social image, while the very act of acknowledgement literally speaks the prohibition. This declaration is not so much a genuine acceptance as it is a mode to practice the opposite: veiling shameful truths. By exaggerating her fantasies she is able to keep her desires at a distance.

More notably, however, is the fact that her predominant fantasy circumscribes the very specificity of Dorsday's condition: that is, the exhibitionistic exposure of her body. She recalls how "intoxicated" she felt when she performed the act of exhibitionism on the balcony in Gmunden (Schnitzler 223). While dressing for dinner in her room she decides to leave the curtains open, thinking it "too bad" that someone is not outside watching her (Schnitzler 204-05). Else finds these acts of exhibitionism exciting, yet it is the possibility of being visible that constitutes her constant paranoia.

Despite Else's powerful preconscious desires for sexual expression, the oppositional efficacy of her superego is evident. For example, she contemplates the appropriate dress for an unmarried bourgeois woman, wishing that her décolletage could be lower, thus acknowledging the transgression of the exposed female body (Schnitzler 204). Furthermore, her response to Dorsday's advances establishes her conflicted position by acknowledging the "indecency" of his proposition, yet she is unable/unwilling to respond to his impropriety. She thinks, "I'd like to call him a beast to his face, but I can't. Or is it that I don't want to?"

(Schnitzler 220). This dissonance is pervasive throughout the novella. She later addresses this dissonance between the act of posing nude for Dorsday and her exaggerated fantasies of promiscuity. She questions her repugnance to his request, thinking, "Oh, Mademoiselle Else, why are you making all this fuss? A minute ago you were prepared to run away, to become the lover of strange men, one after the other. And the trifle that Herr von Dorsday demands of you – that bothers you" (Schnitzler 231). It is clear Else is cognizant of this discord between inclination and aversion. Yet, her thought also stands as a justification for exhibiting her body to Dorsday, as this contemplation is a rationalization that aims to reconcile these aspects of inclination and aversion. She hopes to establish a hierarchy of proscribed deeds, in which the act of posing for Dorsday pales in comparison to those of her fantasies. In disregarding the difference between fantasy and reality, between choice and obligation, she attempts to qualify these transgressions in an order that justifies her exhibition for Dorsday. Her efforts to convince herself of the similarities between these two forms of expression underscore how fundamentally different they are.

Else's superego has internalized the negative conceptualization of female sexuality in *fin-de-siècle* Vienna. Her ambivalence should thus be read in relation to this social context. Carl Schorske notes that Vienna's bourgeois culture was consistent with that of Victorian Europe in general: "Morally, [Vienna] was secure, righteous, and repressive" (6). Decadence and hedonism carried repercussions. Traditional mores, constructed ideations of conscience, were steadfastly ingrained in the collective psyche. Any indulgence in pleasure was inseparable from the internalized moral culture of law. This is not to say that the bourgeois class was not sexually inclined. Rather, the moral law was dictated by prohibitions. As Peter Gay notes,

> [I]f the bourgeois motto is self-abnegation, that is not because their passions are feeble but because their passions are harnessed – in Freud's word, 'refined' – in ways that those of coarse peasants or laborers, or for that matter self-indulgent aristocrats, are not. (26)

In other words, the bourgeoisie was a particularly repressive class. It is this heightened repressive functionality that establishes a greater capacity for psychical conflict vis-à-vis sexuality. Else stands as an ideal case study, as she embodies the ambivalence of Viennese modernism. She longs for autonomy, yet defers to the patriarchal structure. She desires sexual expression, yet defers to social prescriptions for a bourgeois female. Her repressive nature is shown as she stifles thoughts of sexual expression when they enter her consciousness. Nevertheless, sexuality and sexual openness were definitive elements of Viennese modernism (Luft 41). This is an essential paradox of turn-of-the-century Viennese subjectivity. Incompatible images of sexuality presented "conceptual chaos" (Kaye 53). Else's thoughts reflect this paradoxical chaos. She reproaches Dorsday's advances as indecent, yet professes, "I'm a slut" (Schnitzler 223). By identifying herself as a "slut," she articulates her desire, yet this identification is restricted to the symbolic structure of language, which demarcates the bourgeois female body of *fin-de-siècle* Vienna. Else is forced to negotiate her own demands amidst the ambiguity of social prohibition and permissiveness, as well as the restrictive indebtedness of the female body.

The Indebtedness of the Female Body

The request for the exhibitionistic act systematically coincides with an unspoken indebtedness of the female body to the male desire that constitutes the social order. Else's mother acknowledges Dorsday's "interest" in Else, and she utilizes the familial debt, with the understanding that Dorsday will, in turn, call upon the corporeal debt of the female body, an indebtedness to the patriarchal social structure. As Dorsday says, "even thirty thousand gulden have to be earned" (216). Incidentally, he is standing near Else, who is seated on a bench, when he says this, with his foot up on the bench. He resumes a "respectable stance" when two women pass by (216-17). Dorsday is making advances towards Else. He sees her request for money as an opportunity for exploitation. The question becomes: what means could Else possess to earn this money?

Dorsday's expectation is for payment of a sexual nature, as is dictated by his unrespectable stance coupled with the requisition that the money be earned. This expectation of corporeal payment is structured, and thus facilitated, by the systematic lack of female income. Else is unmarried and is supported financially by her father. A respectable bourgeois woman did not work outside the home. It is her lack of income, as a result of her gender, that puts her in the position to be used as payment. She laments, "Oh God, why don't I have any money?" (Schnitzler 202). The answer is, of course, that she is a young bourgeois woman. Dorsday states that the money must be earned, because he knows, just as her parents know, that her social status limits her means to earn this money. Without her own finances, Else is seen as an object, always available for purchase or trade. Therefore, both her father (via the mother) and Dorsday deem the exposure of her body to be an axiomatic recourse. It can thus be read as a social contract, in which men appropriate the female body as a mode of exchange. This also speaks to Else's identification as a "slut," because this mode of exchange is socially allowed, yet when a woman exercises independence regarding her sexuality, it becomes a social taboo.

If the parents are, in fact, anticipating the sexual terms of Dorsday's request, then they offer Else's body as compensation, as bait. She is not the intermediary of debt repayment; she, or more specifically, her body, is the currency. It is imbued with a concrete monetary value – fifty thousand gulden. It is noteworthy that in the first letter Else's mother claims the debt is for thirty thousand gulden, but later Else receives another telegram stressing that the "sum [is] not thirty, but fifty" (237). The destination, or rather recipient, a doctor named Fiala, has not changed, yet this increase adds suspicion to the mother's request. Perhaps Fiala has demanded more money or the father has since accrued more debt, or perhaps the parents are seeking more money after having decided their daughter can obtain more than thirty thousand gulden. The change in sum mostly adds to the suspicious nature of the parental request, attributing more validity to Else's mistrust of their intentions.

Nevertheless, her body is imbued with a monetary value, established by Dorsday's condition and designated by the sum set forth by the parents. This quantification of her body qualifies her conceptual status as a "slut." The social structure, of which the parents and Dorsday are instruments, prostitutes the female body. Following his request, Dorsday both acknowledges and denies this exploitation:

> Yes, I say 'request', even if it seems despairingly like extortion. But I'm not an extortionist; I'm just a man who has learned many things from experience – among them this: that everything in the world has its price and that anyone who gives his money away when he is in a position to get something for it is a consummate fool. And – what I want to buy now, Else, as valuable as it is, won't make you any poorer if you sell it. And that it would remain a secret between you and me, this I swear to you, Else, by – by all the charms whose revelation will make me happy. (Schnitzler 220-21)

Dorsday exculpates himself by claiming his request to be a necessary part of the structural order. He is an extortionist, however, due precisely to his appropriation of that structure, and his position in reference to Else's. His justification is typical, in that the economic system demands return, which lends itself to the patriarchal system of exchange. He acknowledges the value of her body, but rejects the possibility that its purchase could negatively impact the product (her body), and fails to recognize its inseparability from her person, that is, from her sense-of-self. Yet, if this transaction did not have the capacity to affect the self in this manner,

Dorsday would not need to ensure its secrecy. He assumes that damage to the female self occurs only in its publicity, emphasizing that value is tied to notions of honor and shame, which are weighed and defined within the public scope.

Dorsday's original justification for his conditional request is neither economic nor pragmatic, but rather attempts to remove his agency entirely: "I'm only a man after all. And it's not my fault that you're so beautiful, Else" (219). This construct of the female as an object of temptation proposes that "even when women are silent (or verbalizing exactly the opposite), their bodies are seen as 'speaking' a language of provocation" (Bordo 6). Dorsday's two justifications speak to the sexual desires of men and the economic position to pursue these desires. Else's body and sense of self are trapped within an ambiguous patriarchal structure, which demands in private that which it condemns in public. These demands are possible because men are "in a position to get something" (Schnitzler 220).

Else's monologue illuminates her position both on and in this structure, as she conceptualizes her interactions with men to be that of constant exchange, in which her body takes on objective and/or monetary value:

> Paul, if you give me the thirty thousand, you can have anything you want from me. No, that's right out of a novel again. The noble daughter sells herself for her beloved father, and in the end really enjoys it. Ugh, disgusting! No, Paul, even for thirty thousand you can't have me. No one can. But for a million? – For a palace? For a string of pearls? If I marry some day, I'll probably do it for less. Is that really so bad? (Schnitzler 203-204)

Else, too, turns to the prostitution of her body as the obvious solution to matters of finance. Her oscillating thoughts once again underscore the blurring of desire and necessity, where she molds the apparent imperative for the solicitation of her body into an absurdly romanticized version of that reality. Within this fantasy she possesses control over the terms of her solicitation, yet even within her realm of fantasy she cannot escape the socially defined spaces of the female body. She has internalized the exploitative structure that limits women to sexual avenues of exchange, and therefore also operates within this framework.

Furthermore, *Fräulein Else* exemplifies Schnitzler's belief that marriage is a microcosm, defined by masculinity, which failed to consider matters of female sexuality (Oosterhoff 131). The topic of marriage is one that Else turns to throughout the novella. In the previous quote, Else notes the masculine exploitation of the female body as inherent to the institution of marriage. Ute Frevert emphasizes that "women possessed no money of their own, were not able to dispose of their property themselves and were therefore dependent on their husbands for everything they wanted or needed" (44). Else feels that marriage is yet another financial contract, in which the female body stands as currency, and sex defines female livelihood. She views marriage as an auction, where beautiful women are more valuable. She aims to justify the sale of her body to Dorsday by acknowledging the inevitability of such an exchange. Her attempt at rational justification illustrates the complexity of her sexual dissonance.

To read the request of exhibition as congruent with Else's subjective fantasy is to disregard the social structures of power. In this sense, regardless of Else's desire for exhibitionism, the fantasy dissolves in its realization within the process of exploitation. It can be argued that dropping her coat in the music room is an act of sexual autonomy, yet this is a moment of defiance. It is not a matter of pleasure, but concerns rather the nullification of displeasure. Her fantasy cannot be realized amidst patriarchal exploitation. The fantasy of exhibitionism is dependent upon autonomy and negated by obligation.

This exploitation of women as a medium of exchange presupposes a relational lack. Such transactions operate within a patriarchal system that lacks the symbolic signification of female identity. This is the type of symbolic identification that Judith Butler underscores in her dialogue with Lévi-Strauss and Jacques Lacan in *Gender Trouble*. Else can be seen as a "relational term," which carries a symbolic masculine identity in her transference between the father and Dorsday (Butler 52). Her female body is the site of patriarchal exchange. It is a reflection not of feminine, but of masculine desires, and is therefore said to *be* the Phallus, whereas the masculine object *has* the Phallus (Butler 62). Thus, the act of exhibitionism is not the autonomous display of female desire. It is the exposure of the feminine lack, the exposure of the female body as a symbolic object containing masculine desire.

The constitution of the patriarchal structure demands the female body as a site of reflection, while its reconstitution requires the social participation of the female subject. Not only does Else act as instrument to the patriarchal structure by exposing her body, but other female characters contribute directly to the substantiation of that structure, and thus assume the role of masculine proxy. Most notable are Else's mother and Frau Cissy, another young woman vacationing in Martino di Castrozza, who competes with Else for the attention of Else's cousin, Paul .

As noted, it is the mother who sends the request in the place of the father, and in doing so willingly offers her daughter as payment. The mother submits Else to the systemic exploitation by Herr von Dorsday, whereas Frau Cissy verbally shames Else following the act of exhibitionism. As Else lies "unconscious" on the bed, Cissy whispers to her:

> Do you know what you did, Else? Just think, you came into the music room dressed only in your coat and suddenly you stood there naked in front of everyone and then you fainted. An hysterical attack, everyone says. I don't believe a word of it. I don't believe you're really unconscious, either. I bet you can hear every word I'm saying. (Schnitzler 259)

Frau Cissy antagonizes Else while laughing about the situation. By accusing Else of being conscious, she literally denies Else's unconsciousness, not only the state of unconsciousness, but also the unconscious (in the psychoanalytic sense) aspect to her behavior. By maintaining Else's consciousness, Cissy marginalizes her in accordance to the rules of the social order regarding the female body. This consciousness finds location in spaces of visibility, where it may be shamed. The two female characters, the mother and Cissy, thus substantiate the dichotomy of private and public to the extent that the mother speaks to the hidden, private truths of the social order, while Cissy adheres to the outward hypocrisy of social propriety.

Although Else's sense of familial obligation and desire to maintain her bourgeois lifestyle informs her compliance in seeking Dorsday's aid, she remains the external locus for the convergence of masculine desires. Her fantasy of exposing herself is constructed around an inverse position of power. Yet, the formation of this fantasy presupposes the indebtedness of the female body, as the latter precludes the actualization of the former. Due to this autonomous lack, as Lorna Martens notes, the pleasure in the exposure of this body further subordinates the female body to the structure of patriarchal power (121-122). Else cannot reappropriate the signification of her body, because the symbolic order is a masculine dictation, and the very attempt at reappropriation carries negative signification. She cannot assume pleasure in the exhibition of her body, because it is subjected in its reflection of masculine desire/power. Her body is subordinated in a signified relationship that embodies the "slave morality" of Lacanian theory (Butler 77). The understanding of the relationship between the sexes as predicated on subjection was already firmly in place during Schnitzler's life, as thinkers like Robert Owen and John Stuart Mill drew analogies to slavery, and underscored the reciprocity of despotism in the public and private spheres (Folbre 193-96). Else, too, acknowledges her position, thinking "[…] Herr von Dorsday bids his slave to dance naked" (Schnitzler 230). Thus, Else understands her act of exhibitionism as a performance in which masculine desire orchestrates the subordination of the female body. Just as her indebtedness to the father marks her mother's request as an imperative, without money of her own, Dorsday's request, too, becomes an imperative. She is indebted to the patriarchal system; that is, she is enslaved.

Conclusion

Else's body is objectified as capital and serves as payment for the relational appeasement of male desire. Her subjective demands for the expression of sexuality clash with social proscriptions, and her identity formation, with regard to female sexuality, remains void of autonomous representation amidst the symbolic signification of the female body in the patriarchal Law. Else's conflicting psychical, social, and familial obligations circumscribe the indebtedness of the female body, and obviate the autonomous identification of this body. The indebtedness of the female body defines the inevitability of Else's ego to fail to meet intrapsychic and interpsychic demands. Butler asserts that, "The construction of the law that guarantees failure is symptomatic of a slave morality that disavows the very generative powers it uses to construct the 'Law' as a permanent impossibility" (77). There is truth, then, in Else's claim that "Herr von Dorsday bids his slave to dance naked" (Schnitzler 230). Not only is she obligated to expose her body to him, but also the order, or 'Law,' that dictates this obligation governs the impossibility for subversion. The resolution of Else's conflict is unattainable within the patriarchal social order.

For Else, her irreconcilable debts and inability to establish an identity outside the systematic prescriptions for a woman in *fin-de-siècle* Vienna determine her fate. The repetition of "Address remains Fiala," reiterates the perpetual and inevitable indebtedness of the female body. It also speaks to Else's subjective fate: suicide. She admits, "I'm not cut out for bourgeois life […] Whether at nineteen or at twenty-one, it doesn't make any difference" (233-34). Else blames the social order for this inevitability, asserting that her death "would serve them right, every one of them; they've raised me only to sell myself, in one way or another […] All of you are guilty for my having turned out this way, not only Papa and Mama" (230-31).

The result of Else's conflict is the self-destruction of this indebted body. By committing suicide she destroys the ego that failed to satisfy conflicting demands, while violently rejecting the social order that prostitutes her. There is no possibility for her body to be exposed in her own terms. Her debt to oppositional coordinates in the constellation of her dissonance leaves her, quite simply, doomed, with no escape from the inevitable: a violent reaction against both the self and the social bond. Her debts are irreconcilable. Ultimately, she pays a heavy price to free herself from the indebtedness of the female body. "Address remains Fiala."

Works Cited

Bordo, Susan. *Unbearable Weight: Feminism, Western Culture, and the Body*. Berkeley: U. of California P., 1993. Print.
Butler, Judith. *Gender Trouble: Feminism and the Subversion of Identity*. New York: Routledge, 2006. Print.
Folbre, Nancy. *Greed, Lust & Gender: A History of Economic Ideas*. Oxford: Oxford U.P., 2009. Print.
Freud, Sigmund. *An Outline of Psycho-Analysis*. New York: W.W. Norton, 1969. Print.
Frevert, Ute. *Women in German History: From Bourgeois Emancipation to Sexual Liberation*. Trans. Stuart McKinnon-Evans. New York: Berg, 1989. Print.
Gay, Peter. *Schnitzler's Century: The Making of Middle-Class Culture, 1815-1914*. New York: W.W. Norton, 2002. Print.
Kaye, Richard A. "Sexual Identity at the Fin de Siècle." *The Cambridge Companion to the Fin de Siècle*. Ed. Gail Marshall. 53-72. New York: Cambridge U.P., 2007. Print.
Luft, David S. *Eros and Inwardness in Vienna: Weininger, Musil, Doderer*. Chicago: U of Chicago P, 2003. Print.
Martens, Lorna. "Naked Bodies in Schnitzler's Late Prose." *Die Seele... ist ein wites Land: Kritische Beiträge zum Werk Arthur Schnitzlers*. Ed., Joseph P. Strelka. New York: Peter Lang, 1996. pp. 107-129. Print.
Oosterhoff, Jenneke A. *Die Männer sind infam, solang sie Männer sind: Konstruktionen der Männlichkeit in den Werken Arthur Schnitzlers*. Tübingen: Stauffenburg Verlag, 2000. Print.
Schorske, Carl E. *Fin-de-Siècle Vienna: Politics and Culture*. New York: Alfred A. Knopf, 1980. Print.
Schnitzler, Arthur. "Fräulein Else." *Desire and Delusion: Three Novellas*. Ed. Margret   Schaefer. Chicago: Ivan R. Dee, 2003. Print.
Skeggs, Beverley. *Formations of Class and Gender: Becoming Respectable*. London: Sage, 1997. Print.

CHAPTER FOUR

UNBINDING THE TRAGIC "DREAM" OF HUMAN ABJECTION: PAYING THE DEBT OF GENDER-BASED ABJECTION IN NEIL GAIMAN'S *THE SANDMAN*

MARY CATHERINE HARPER

> Representation mingles with what it represents . . . one thinks as if the represented were nothing more than the shadow or reflection of the representer. A dangerous promiscuity and a nefarious complicity between the reflection and the reflected which lets itself be seduced narcissistically.
> (Jacques Derrida, *Of Grammatology* 36)

The tragic visions of Classical, Renaissance, and Modern drama enjoy distinctive characteristics. For example, the four major tragic heroes of Shakespeare—Hamlet, Othello, Lear, and Macbeth—examine a complex rational yet often self-contradictory and confused Subject who is compelled to examine his behavior self-consciously and take responsibility for the consequences of his actions. King Lear is a prime example: after he has used and abused the natural love-bond between father and child for self-serving political aims, he realizes his folly. A representation of tragedy's characteristic wisdom-come-too-late, Lear indicts himself in a frank discussion about a barking dog: "There thou mightst behold the great image of authority: a dog's obeyed in office" (*King Lear* 4.6.157-59). Even Macbeth, often misinterpreted as the pawn of Fate clothed in the figure of three witches or the pawn of his wife, admits just after meeting the witches and well before his wife counsels him to murder King Duncan that his own natural tendency is toward "horrible imaginings" (*Macbeth* 1.3.139). He transforms the witches' prophecy that he will be king into the "horrid image" of regicide (*Macbeth* 1.3.136). Shortly after, he settles into the truth of the matter, that "I have no spur / To prick the sides of my intent, but only / Vaulting ambition, which o'erleaps itself / And falls on th'other" (*Macbeth* 1.7.25-28).

Renaissance Shakespearean tragedy thus includes human agency in political, social, and personal arenas. But 2000 years earlier, in Classical Greek drama, the tragic hero is typically faced with a choice between accepting or trying to escape that which cannot be escaped: Destiny, or Fate. The classic example is Oedipus, who stabs out his own eyes when faced with the knowledge of fulfilling the destiny he has attempted to escape. Rather than resign himself to having by destiny killed his father and sired children by his own mother, he rails against the god of his destiny. In the Berkowitz/Brunner translation of Sophocles's *Oedipus Tyrannus*, when asked by the chorus why he has stabbed out his eyes— "How could you blind yourself? What demon drove you?"—Oedipus replies, "Apollo! It was Apollo! *He* brought this pain, this suffering to me. But it was my own hand that struck the blow. Not his. O God! Why should I have sight when all that I would see is ugliness?" (30). Here is the assertion of human agency against greater cosmic forces.

At the other end of the history of dramatic (or literary) tragedy, skepticism about human agency shakes the Humanistic foundations of Renaissance tragedy and gives way to the ironic, behavioristic vision the 20th century, with its elements of the literary form of Grotesque and of farce. Plays such as *Long Day's Journey into Night*, with its drug-addicted mother no less trapped by obsessive-compulsive behavior than any other member of her family, and *Waiting for Godot*, a prime example of Theater of the Absurd, are part of the shift from tragic vision to ironic play with what is variously called the Subject, Ego, or Agent. These and other Modern texts not only serve to critique tragedy as a form of dramatic narrative but, also, the foundational Classical belief in heroics.

Today, in what is being called the postmodern period by literary critics and cultural theorists, the ideas of "Tragedy" and "tragic hero" have been transformed into self-reflexive "play." Even one of Shakespeare's tragedies—*Hamlet*—has been presented as an engagement with a meta-discursive "house of mirrors" where the central character, as "played" by Kenneth Branagh, toys with the idea of agency as a self-conscious performance. In this postmodern interpretation of the play, human agency in the form of the character Hamlet is a mere something acted out in front of a set of mirrors, something always brutally honest with itself yet having no core truth nor any external referent against which to judge or even interpret action.

Still, in the midst of the over-determined self-illumination and playful "Self" doubt of our postmodern condition, there may be something of heroics, something akin to a tragic vision, something that makes the "examined life" of a "tragic hero" matter. This is no trivial matter, for literature still appears to serve that cultural function of turning the "mirror" this way and that upon the human Subject, still asking how sure we are even of our border-crossing, multi-positional postmodern identities. Literatures of various sorts continue to serve the question of why seeming Subjects with seeming agency are still wrestling with what appear to be abject Objects before the "mirror." Neil Gaiman's serial novel called *The Sandman* does just that, especially emphasizing reconfigured gender relations that change the rules of the Subject/Abject game. Generally speaking, the central character of *The Sandman*, Morpheus, questions attitudes about gender in his long tale of fateful and tragic heroics. And one of the theories that obviously grounds Morpheus's self-examination is Julia Kristeva's theory of abjection. She asserts:

> The abject is the violence of mourning for an "object" that has always already been lost. The abject shatters the wall of repression and its judgments. It takes the ego back on its source in the abominable limits from which, in order to be, the ego has broken away—it assigns it a source in the non-ego, drive, and death. Abjection is a resurrection that has gone through death (of the ego). It is an alchemy that transforms death drive into a start of life, of new significance. (*Powers of Horror* 15)

This passage alludes to the gender-troubling structures and processes still evident in postmodern life and points to, using a term from Tragedy studies, a potential for *denouement*, for "unraveling" those structures and processes.

So too for the binding of the "tragic knot" of abjection and unraveling of it by Morpheus as he pays his "gender-debt" in Neil Gaiman's postmodern *Sandman* graphic novel. The first 75 episodes—the first ten volumes—of what amounts to a 1850-page serial novel present the emotional maturation and fated tragic death of Morpheus, a character who goes by "Dream" ("Oneiros" or "Kai'ckul") in more than one language and has several titles: "Lord of the Dreaming," the "Dream King," and "Morpheus of the Endless." As one of the seven Endless siblings— manifestations of the human elements of Destiny, Death, Dream, Destruction, Desire, Despair, Delight-who-is-now-Delirium, in that order of "birth" in the story's cosmography—Morpheus exists to regulate the sleeping dream life of humans. He enters *Preludes and Nocturnes*, the first volume of the novel cloaked in a black-as-night Goth costume to signify the Office of Dream. He seems to be an allegorical figure, figuratively cloaked as it were in the obligation to create and deliver dreams to the human community.

In the first volume, just as Morpheus's role as the creator (or manifestation) of the human dream world is established, he is imprisoned by a necromancer's spell that has gone awry. The point of the spell was to trap and gain power over Dream's big sister Death, but circumstances bring Morpheus into the conjuring. According to the opening plot, for almost a century, from 1916 to 1988, Morpheus remains trapped in a dome-like "cage" and is, thus, unable to tend to the Dreaming, resulting in a "sleepy sickness" across the world (*Preludes and Nocturnes*, "Sleep of the Just").[1] His imprisonment gives Morpheus much time to plan revenge on his captors. After freeing himself, he does not tend immediately to the Dreaming, which has fallen into a state of chaos with some dreamscapes breaking out of their normal boundaries and a few dangerous nightmares escaping into the human waking world. Instead, Morpheus sets out to revenge himself on Alex Burgess, the son of the now-dead necromancer. He places Alex in a state of "eternal waking," which is essentially a neverending nightmare from which he cannot wake (*Preludes and Nocturnes*, "Sleep of the Just"). In treating Alex as a vanquished enemy, Morpheus is, in effect, failing in his duty to serve all of humanity. Eventually he will make amends for his transgression against Alex, but that is much later, after the narrative takes Morpheus into contact with several female characters he has heretofore treated poorly, taking license with his office and powers.

At this point in the story he finally returns to the Dreaming and finds that his three objects—helmet, ruby, and sandbag—are missing. His helmet, the symbol of the Dream Lord's office, has been taken by the humans and passed onto a demon of Hell. His two basic tools—a ruby power stone and the traditional bag of sand that the "Sandman" uses to bring humans into the Dreaming—have also been taken. After some detective work, Morpheus realizes he has to travel to Hell, the realm of Lucifer Morningstar, and there he comes face to face with a woman in a cage, tears in her eyes, begging to be freed by Morpheus. Recognizing her, he replies coldly to the woman, Nada, that he has not yet forgiven her. The story of Nada is not given in *Preludes and Nocturnes*; rather, there is only a reference to Nada having died and been sent to Hell some 10,000 years before (*Preludes and Nocturnes*, "A Hope in Hell").

In *The Doll's House*, volume two of *Sandman*, the story of Nada is told. She is queen of an African city-state, a city of glass and light thriving at the beginning of the agricultural revolution. Morpheus comes to

---

[1] Only one of *The Sandman* volumes, *The Wake*, has normal pagination, so except for references to that volume, in-text citation will include only volume title and available chapter title or number.

Nada in her dreams. She falls in love with him, and he invites her to give up her earthly realm and join him in his Endless Dreaming. But Nada wants only to remain a live human, ruling her city, serving her people. While she loves Kai'ckul/Dream, She reminds him that "it is not given to mortals to love the Endless" (*The Doll's House*, "Prologue: Tales in the Sand"). Still, she allows herself to be seduced, and the effect is the destruction of her city:

> When the sun arose that morning, and saw the two of them together, it knew . . . and a blazing fireball fell from the sun and burnt up the city of glass, razing it to the ground, leaving just a desert. . . . Nada saw the sun throw down the fireball, saw her city melt, saw her land become a parched wasteland. (*The Doll's House*, "Prologue: Tales in the Sand")

Failing to protect the inhabitants of her city, Nada commits suicide. And Kai'ckul's response? Ignoring the destruction he has helped cause, he gives now-dead Nada three chances to join him in the Dreaming. When Nada refuses him a first, second, and then third time, Kai'ckul /Morpheus condemns her to Hell in an arrogant rage (*The Doll's House*, "Prologue: Tales in the Sand").

This is the first instance of Morpheus's bad behavior toward females alluded to in the exposition or detailed in the novel's plot. Each time this happens, he essentially abandons his duties to humankind to pursue an object of his personal desire. His womanizing is evidence of a tragic flaw, a self-involved disregard for humans that reduces them to abject objects and results in an accumulation of "debt" that will one day come due. Such transgression having been set in motion by his own hand, Morpheus's story unfolds in dual fashion: according to the Romance genre (or hero's tale) of meeting a series of trials and restoring societal order; and as a meandering postmodern tragedy in which the tragic figure after thousands of years finally develops an understanding of why he must always exercise his dream powers without arrogance, without coldness, and with full presence and care for the humans he is duty-bound to serve. Morpheus will learn the lesson that he is servant, not master, of humans, but this recognition (or *anagnorisis*) comes slowly.

Along the way Morpheus behaves badly several times over and particularly badly toward females (human and mythic alike): desiring them, encouraging them to fall in love with him, securing their devotion, then tiring of them and returning to his creative task of developing a wide range of dreams for human consumption. Morpheus's behavior is to be expected . . . when we remember that he is, in effect, made of the imaginary stuff of human stories of both daily life and mythology. He is a postmodern figure standing in for and, thus, calling to mind tragic heroes from other periods, like the Renaissance. And a common theme especially in Renaissance tragedy is transgression against The Feminine. Linda Bamber's analysis of Tragedy from a feminist perspective identifies the role of The Feminine in this dramatic form: "The feminine Other creates drama by resisting the hero, but also by being endlessly desirable to him. The desire of the hero for women and the world keeps him both alive and vulnerable; it keeps open the possibility of both suffering and fulfillment" (242). Thus it is for Morpheus and Nada. Though the scene in Hell in which Morpheus refuses to "forgive her" is quite brief, Nada has pricked Morpheus's conscience. She "creates drama" of the relational sort found in Tragedy, not Romance.

And Morpheus's big sister Death pricks his conscience as well, when she accuses Morpheus of doing "a terrible thing to that poor girl" Nada. "You acted appallingly," she says at the beginning of the fourth volume. Repeating their sister Desire's admonishment of Morpheus, she continues: "It *IS* bad news for us to get involved with them [with humans]. You know that. . . . Maybe she didn't *WANT* to be a goddess, Little Brother. Did you ever consider *THAT*?" (*Season of Mists*, "Episode 0: Prologue").

It is in this scene with his sister that Morpheus vows to go to Hell either to free Nada, or to die trying (*Season of Mists*, "Episode 0: Prologue"). Morpheus's vow is significant, not just in terms of the plot or character development but also in relation to the workings of tragic form in the Classical Greek period. Judith Fletcher teases out the importance of the kind of vow Morpheus makes in her study of Euripidean tragedies, where "potent speech acts" allow women who are otherwise powerless "to control men's language and action" (29). Fletcher explains that in ancient Greek society and, thus, in their tragedies, "when men swear to do something for a woman—grant sanctuary, keep a secret, carry a letter—. . . they also enter into a contract with the gods who function as the guarantors of the oath. This triangulated relationship—man, woman, god—contributes to the increased agency of female protagonists" (29-30). Morpheus fulfills his vow to rescue Nada from Hell (*Season of Mists*, "Episode/Chapter 6"), but not without having to exercise patience, diplomacy, even generosity toward a number of troublesome characters, including a few Norse gods including Loki, two Egyptian gods, members of the Fairy folk from Oberon and Titania's court, angels and demons of the Hebraic god, a god of Japan, and manifestations of Order and Chaos, all of them bent on manipulating Morpheus. After freeing Nada, he willingly accepts her "will," to be reincarnated and live another lifetime as a human individual (*Season of Mists*, "Episode ∞: Epilogue").

In giving himself in service to a female, Morpheus makes himself vulnerable to powers outside of his control in the way Linda Bamber means. His service to Nada also calls to mind a structural component of Tragedy that Susanne Langer describes as "The Tragic Rhythm." According to Langer, "the idea of personal Fate was mythically conceived . . . as a mysterious power inherent in the world," part of human nature itself. For any character fated to be a tragic hero, "tragic action is the realization of all his possibilities, which he unfolds and exhausts in the course of the drama. His human nature is his Fate" (114). What this means for Morpheus is that, through the process of freeing Nada, he discovers the better part of himself: the part that exercises thoughtfulness and patience in solving problems, the part that seeks to do no harm to other beings, the servant of those who have need of the Dreaming.

Morpheus's recognition that he is a servant to human imagination and human well being is a direct result of what I would call "trial by gender conflict." In the fifth volume, *A Game of You*, the results of gender abjectification are highlighted as Morpheus attempts to undo the negative consequences of his earlier objectification/abjectification of females. Samuel R. Delany provides analysis of Morpheus's relationship to gender in his preface to that volume, where he reminds us that comics, as a genre, are all about "a fantasy world where the natural forces, stated and unstated, whether of myth or chance, *enforce* the dominant ideology we've got around us today" (*A Game of You*, "Preface"). According to Delany, the dominant ideology still insists on token stories of the death of members of marginalized groups, those heroic abjects—"blacks, women, Asians, gays, or what have you . . . so that we can feel sorry for them, then forget about them" (*A Game of You*, "Preface"). Delany argues that the narratival structure of comics "remains just a nasty fantasy unless, in our reading of it, we can find some irony, something that subverts it, something that resists that fantasy . . . problematizes it" (*A Game of You*, "Preface"). He asserts that Gaiman's novel is full of such "ironic spin," and he suggests that a "wilder and more delirious order of fantasy is let loose" in *A Game of You* upon the culturally dangerous fantasy that "the dominant ideology is not socially constructed but is rather enforced by [some] transcendental order of nature" (*A Game of You*, "Preface"). Delany further argues that a central female character, Thessaly, who is a "centuries-old moon witch," cannot win the gender war that unfolds in the chapters of *A Game of You*. "No one can win the Game of I," he says (*A Game of You*, "Preface").

And I agree. The game of abjection in that "mirror" of the Subject is brought into critical focus in that fifth volume of the novel—literally in focus, too, as represented by mirrors in the first, second, and sixth (or last)

chapters and by the obviousness of Thessaly's over-large glasses. In this
volume Morpheus dismantles a dreamscape he has previously created for
patriarchal females, those who tend to enjoy and support the patriarchal
status quo. One such female is a character named Barbie, now living in
New York City in a culturally diverse apartment building. As Barbie
grows close to lesbian and transgender neighbors, the dreamscape also
changes, turning into a war zone of sorts between the essentialist feminist
Thessaly, whom Delany describes in the preface, and a willful child-avatar
of Barbie who is intent on keeping the patriarchal status quo (*A Game of
You*, "Bad Room Rising," "Beginning to See the Light"). Barbie and a
transgender woman named Wanda become victims of the patriarchal
child-avatar figure, resulting in Wanda's death in the waking world at the
same moment that Morpheus in the Dreaming tries to gentle the "child"
out of her ideological position. She throws a tantrum in her patriarchal
dreamscape, causing the apartment building in the real world to collapse
upon Wanda (*A Game of You*, "Over the Sea to Sky").

Wanda's death by patriarchal tantrum implicates Thessaly, for her
approach is as resistant as the child-avatar's. In the midst of the conflict
between these polarized figures, Morpheus exercises his now-developed
gentleness toward humans and the figures of the Dreaming. Gone is the
self-involved, dismissive, vengeful Morpheus of volume one. However,
Morpheus has a debt to pay, and the tragic consequences of Morpheus's
earlier bad behavior—with more evidence of the "old" Morpheus in *The
Doll's House* (volume two)—are not distinct until much later in the novel,
in *Brief Lives* and *The Kindly Ones* (volumes seven and nine). Although
Morpheus's internal struggle has been, in large part, about that same
masculinist "will to power" that Madelon Gohlke Sprengnether describes
in the context of Shakespearean tragedy (250), the narrative path of the
Morpheus tragedy does not match the narrative structure of *King Lear*,
Othello, and *Macbeth*.[2] In these tragedies, the consequences come swiftly
after, as Sprengnether puts it, "the exercise of power turns against the
hero" (251). In contrast, Gaiman's serial graphic novel allows for the
development of many more story digressions and sub-plots than in
Renaissance Tragedy, which itself contains sub-plots not found in the
Classical or Modernist versions of the genre. And the postmodern
storytelling of Gaiman includes additional flashback elements, with much
evidence of the "old" Morpheus in the flashback sections of *Dream
Country* and *Fables and Reflections* (volumes three and six).

---

[2] *Hamlet*'s narrative structure, with its tragic hero's hesitations and digressions,
might have more in common with the structure of *The Sandman* than with other
Shakespearean tragedies.

This looseness of temporal structure in *The Sandman* may appear a mere playful postmodern anomaly, but it serves a very important effect, and that is to highlight and offer a full experience of the workings of abjection within the novel. By the end of volume ten (*The Wake*), the reader has experienced numerous moments of abjection within what seem to be digressions into several stories of the Dreaming. And the experience is interlaced with the earlier moments of Morpheus's life where his "will to power" results in a Subject/Abject transgression, either that or moments when he pays the debt for an earlier transgression. His stories illustrate and draw readers again and again into recurrences of the state of abjection, as Kristeva describes it:

> There, I am at the border of my condition as a living being. My body extricates itself, as being alive, from that border. Such wastes drop so that I might live, until, from loss to loss, nothing remains in me and my entire body falls beyond the limit—*cadere*, cadaver . . . It is no longer I who expel, "I" is expelled . . . Deprived of world, therefore, I *fall in a faint* . . . [I]n that thing that no longer matches and therefore no longer signifies anything, I behold the breaking down of a world that has erased its borders, fainting away. (*Powers of Horror*, 3-4)

The erasure of borders is a liminal experience that marks the failure of meaning for the autonomous Subject. Morpheus experiences this several times over, in both the "present" time and flashback scenes of the plot.

A particularly poignant set of abjection experiences involves Morpheus's wife Calliope and his son Orpheus. *Sandman* draws on the Greek myth of Dream (Oneiros) mating with the muse of epic poetry, Calliope, and fathering Orpheus. In *Fables and Reflections* (volume six) the story of the marriage of Orpheus and Euridice is told, with the conflict between Calliope and her then-demanding and arrogant husband Oneiros/Morpheus as the backdrop. When Euridice is killed by snakebite and taken to Hades, Morpheus urges Orpheus to forget her, saying in his characteristically blunt, dismissive manner, "You are mortal: it is the mortal way. You attend the funeral, you bid the dead farewell. You grieve. Then you continue with your life. . . . She is dead. You are alive. So live" (*Fables and Reflections*, "The Song of Orpheus: Chapter Two"). Of course Orpheus doesn't listen to his father, and we know how the myth of Orpheus and Euridice ends. In the *Fables and Reflections* version of the story, after Orpheus has been savagely dismembered by the Maenads, Morpheus takes the living head of his son and arranges to have it secreted away to an island temple (*Fables and Reflections*, "The Song of Orpheus: Epilogue"). In an especially imaginative chapter set during the French Revolution of the late 1700s, Orpheus's head is caught up in a

Robespierrean purge of religion, mythology, and faith-based artifacts, but Morpheus has Orpheus's head rescued (*Fables and Reflections*, "Thermidor"). In volume seven when Orpheus asks his father to end what is left of his "life," his consciousness, Morpheus obliges, enlisting the aid of his sister Death (*Brief Lives*, "Chapter 9").

This is the act that will set in motion Morpheus's final ordeal as a tragic hero. He will be hounded by the Erinyes for his transgression against the ancient natural law that prohibits murder of a family member. Here is an allusion to the Tragedy cycle *Oresteia*, in which Orestes murders his mother in retribution for her murdering his father, Agamemnon, and is mentally tortured by the Erinyes (the Furies) until Athena restores order and establishes the Erinyes as the Eumenides, the "kindly ones." In the case of Morpheus, the debt of the "blood" crime has to be paid, either by the total destruction of the Dreaming or Morpheus's death. *The Kindly Ones* (volume nine) tells the story of Morpheus and the fury of the Erinyes. It is filled with abject characters—a mother whose child has been abducted, a serial killer, the Norse god of chaos Loki, and others—but none more so than Morpheus himself, who must save the abducted child, knowing he is saving the next incarnation of Dream of the Endless. Then he crosses the ultimate border surrounding every living being into that "final sleep," his sister Death as his guide (*The Kindly Ones*, "Chapter 13").

Overall, the Morpheus/Orpheus abjection "knot" is developed out of Morpheus treating his wife Calliope coldly. The debt of Orpheus's transgression against his wife is paid when he frees the muse after she has been trapped, raped, and held against her will (in a 20th-century segment of the story's timeline) by a hack writer who wants the gift of creativity. When Morpheus/Oneiros frees Calliope, she comments, "You have changed, Oneiros. In the old days, you would have left me to rot forever, without turning a hair." Then she asks if he still hates her for leaving him, and he replies, "No, I no longer hate you, Calliope. I have learned much in recent times, and . . ." (*Dream Country*, "Calliope"). Morpheus, it seems, has learned when not to finish a thought. Or perhaps he simply does not know how to apologize.

Abjection and *anagnorisis* both have the quality of an insufficiency of language. And Morpheus may also have learned by the time of this late-20th-century scene that mastery over voice, like mastery over others, only accrues more Subject/Abject debt. He works to avoid repeating the "identification-projection" of the autonomous Subject, as Kristeva would put it (*Strangers to Ourselves* 187). Instead, he grows more reflective, more careful in action, more thoughtful in his speech. Through his troubled relationships with Nada and several other female characters, including a pregnant woman named Lyta (introduced in volume two), Morpheus faces his gender-based scapegoating and generally dismissive behavior toward female characters. In general, he begins to feel more sympathy for humans and focuses on his duties to them. At the end of *The Doll's House* (volume two), he reminds his hermaphroditic sibling Desire—the manifestation of unexamined, uncontrolled desire—that

> We of the endless are the servants of the living—we are NOT their masters. We exist because they know, deep in their hearts, that we exist. When the last living thing has left this universe, then our task will be done. And we do not manipulate them. If anything, they manipulate us. (*The Doll's House*, "Part Seven: Lost Hearts")

This speech, which echoes the condition of a Subject facing internal abjection, is said as much for Morpheus's own sake as for his sibling's, for it is the first of the several moments of *anagnorisis* in the meandering postmodern novel. It is also something of a general critique of the Modern value of autonomy, both individual autonomy and the "collective totality," as Jean-Luc Nancy states it, that is used in the modern world to organize communities (6). *The Sandman*'s way of dealing with abjection may suggest a larger purpose beyond the unfolding of a literary Tragedy, for Morpheus's consciously modified behavior toward humans has the quality of "inclination" that Nancy theorizes in *The Inoperative Community*. According to Nancy, the inclination (from the French *clinamen*) of singular beings toward each other (4) is the operative gesture that *IS* itself community. Applying this to Morpheus, he is a pattern of story-based gestures and inclinations that may be used as a model for disrupting the now-bankrupt Modern Self and collective totality.

Put in this context, Morpheus's tragedy has meaning beyond the development of an individual character (although character still matters in relation to the aesthetics of the Tragedy genre). What is at stake is not just the debt that one character pays so that he may be redeemed, but the way in which a new idea of human community may be dreamed of. In *The Sandman* the new way is contingent on the investiture of the "Dream" child called Daniel, the son of Lyta (or the Greek Hippolyta). This child will replace the flawed and struggling Morpheus, whose relationship to Daniel's mother Lyta is as important as the Morpheus/Calliope relationship because Lyta figures into the *denouement* of the novel's Tragedy plot. She appears first in *The Doll's House* (volume two) as one of the characters trapped in a dream state during Morpheus's incarceration. When he comes to free her, she mistakenly thinks Morpheus has killed her husband, Hector, who has fallen victim to nightmare figures that have escaped from the Dreaming. Morpheus, too busy with restoring his authority to comfort a mere grieving woman who happens to be pregnant, fails to take the time to explain that Hector did not die by Morpheus's hand. Lyta is left to feel a helpless rage toward Morpheus, and it is made worse when Morpheus further dismisses Lyta by casually informing her that her dream of being pregnant is, in fact, part of waking reality. He also fails to explain that the child, having been conceived in the Dreaming by essentially a ghost father—Hector—means that the child belongs to and is part of Dreaming structure. When Morpheus cavalierly says, "That child is mine. Take good care of it. One day I will come for it," he pulls Lyta into the tragic knot. Lyta screams back, "You take my child over my dead body, you spooky bastard" (*The Doll's House*, "Part Three: Playing House"), a vow that brings Lyta and Morpheus into the fateful conflict in the ninth volume, *The Kindly Ones*.

The vow that Lyta makes is no mere rhetoric. It is a speech act (as defined by J. L. Austin), a piece of performative language of the type that Judith Fletcher discusses in "Women and Oaths in Euripides." Fletcher's argument (above) is that agency was afforded a woman in Greek society by a man's vow to do something for her, and I would add that a woman's own direct vow is also a form of person-to-person agency. In the Morpheus/Lyta relationship, she exercises that agency when her son, Daniel, is abducted by Loki and Puck, and they deceive her into thinking Morpheus has killed the child. She calls on the Erinyes to avenge what she thinks is Daniel's murder and they, in turn, manipulate her to help them destroy the Dreaming as revenge for Morpheus taking the life of his son (*The Kindly Ones*, "Part Three," "Part Seven," "Part Eleven"). And Morpheus's agency? He and his sister Death agree that he is without choice, and at this moment he is bound to die in order to save the Dreaming (*The Kindly Ones*, "Part Thirteen"). In effect, being bound as an Abject by his Endless function and structure, Morpheus has been performing what only *appears* to be agency. The debt is all there is, and the recognition of this is the critical moment of any Tragedy.

But Morpheus is written beyond his tragic end. In masterful postmodern fashion Morpheus offers us another moment of *anagnorisis*, and it is a particularly fine meta-discursive moment because it takes place *after* his death, after his wake, in the final chapter of volume ten, the last of the volumes telling Morpheus's story. In a 1610-11 flashback called "The Tempest," Will Shakespeare asks why the second play that Morpheus has commissioned of him—the first being *A Midsummer Night's Dream*—is not "something lofty, something dark, a tale of a noble hero with a tragic flaw?" Morpheus replies, "I wanted a tale of graceful ends. I wanted a play about a king who drowns his books, and breaks his staff, and leaves his kingdom. About a magician who becomes a man. About a man who turns his back on magic" (181). When Will asks why he wanted this particular story, Morpheus replies, "Because I will never leave my island . . . I am not a man. And I do not change. . . . I do not. I MAY not. I am Prince of stories, Will; but I have no story of my own. Nor shall I ever" (182). As Dream Lord, Morpheus has been both representer and the represented in his already-always empty Subject space. And we are left to remember how we began this reading, cautioned that agency is complicit with abjection. And like a dream, only as solid as we readers choose to make it.

Works Cited

Bamber, Linda. "The Woman Reader in *King Lear.*" *William Shakespeare: The Tragedy of King Lear.* Ed. Russell Fraser. Newly revised ed. New York: Signet Classic-Penguin, 1998. 235-44. Print.

Bevington, David, ed. *The Complete Works of Shakespeare.* 6th ed. New York: Pearson-Longman, 2009. Print.

Delany, Samuel R. "Skerries of the Dream: A Preface." *The Sandman: A Game of You.* Neil Gaiman. Fully remastered ed. Vol. 5. 1991-92, episodes 32-37. New York: DC Comics, 2011. n.p. Print.

Derrida, Jacques. *Of Grammatology.* Trans. Gayatri Chakravorty Spivak. 1976. Corrected ed. Baltimore: Johns Hopkins UP, 1997. Print.

Gaiman, Neil. *The Sandman: Brief Lives.* Vol. 7. 1992-93, episodes 41-49. New York: Vertigo-DC Comics, 1994. Print.

—. *The Sandman: The Doll's House.* Fully recolored ed. Vol. 2. 1989-90, episodes 9-16. New York: DC Comics, 2010. Print.

—. *The Sandman: Dream Country.* Fully recolored ed. Vol. 3. 1990, episodes 17-20. New York: DC Comics, 2010. Print.

—. *The Sandman: Fables and Reflections.* Fully remastered ed. Vol. 6. 1991-93, episodes 29-31, 38-40, 50. New York: DC Comics, 2011. Print.

—. *The Sandman: A Game of You.* Neil Gaiman. Fully remastered ed. Vol. 5. 1991-92, episodes 32-37. New York: DC Comics, 2011. Print.

—. *The Sandman: The Kindly Ones.* Vol. 9. 1993-95, episodes 57-69. New York: Vertigo-DC Comics, 1996. Print.

—. *The Sandman: Preludes and Nocturnes.* Fully recolored ed. Vol. 1. 1988-89, episodes 1-8. New York: DC Comics, 2010. Print.

—. *The Sandman: Season of Mists*. Neil Gaiman. Fully remastered ed. Vol. 4. 1990-91, episodes 21-28. New York: DC Comics, 2010. Print.

—. *The Sandman: The Wake*. Vol. 10. 1995-96, episodes 70-75. New York: Vertigo-DC Comics, 1997. Print.

Fletcher, Judith. "Women and Oaths in Euripides." *Theatre Journal* 55.1 Ancient Theatre (2003): 29-44. *JSTOR*. Web. 8 Oct. 2012. Print.

Kristeva, Julia. *Powers of Horror: An Essay on Abjection*. Trans. Leon S. Roudiez. New York: Columbia UP, 1982. Print.

—. *Strangers to Ourselves*. Trans. Leon S. Roudiez. New York: Columbia UP, 1991. Print.

Langer, Susanne. "The Tragic Rhythm." *Tragedy: Vision and Form*. Ed. Robert W. Corrigan. 2nd ed. (from *Feeling and Form*. New York: Charles Scribner's Sons, 1953. 351-66.) New York: Harper & Row, 1981. 113-23. Print.

Nancy, Jean-Luc. *The Inoperative Community*. Minneapolis: U of Minnesota P, 1991. Print. Theory and History of Literature 76. Print.

Sophocles. *Oedipus Tyrannus*. Trans. Luci Berkowitz and Theodore F. Brunner. 1966. New York: W. W. Norton, 1970. Print.

Shakespeare, William. *King Lear*. Bevington. 1201-54.

—. *Macbeth*. Bevington. 1255-92.

Sprengnether, Madelon Gohlke. "'I wooed thee with my sword': Shakespeare's Tragic Paradigms." *William Shakespeare: The Tragedy of Othello: The Moor of Venice*. Ed. Alvin Kernan. New revised ed. New York: Signet Classic-Penguin, 1986. 245-69. Print.

CHAPTER FIVE

THE LAND AND THE HUMAN BODY IN CORMAC MCCARTHY'S *THE ROAD*: THE IMPORTANCE OF MORAL VALUES IN HUMAN CONNECTION AND BONDING

MANDY CHI MAN LO

The post-apocalyptic world depicted in *The Road*, which recounts the story of a nameless father and his son's journey in the darkened world after a major catastrophe, is a "world shrinking down about a raw core of parsible entities" (McCarthy 93). Apocalyptic events are "understood to destroy functional government, food distribution, organized medical care and the infrastructure on which we rely for most of what we do" (Curtis 2). Similarly, in the world of despair and dispersal in *The Road*, "[t]he names of things slowly following those things into oblivion. Colors. The names of birds. Things to eat. Finally the names of things one believed to be true" (McCarthy 93) are forgotten. People's beliefs, the practiced systems, and organized institutions are all reduced to survival aims. The obliteration of the fundamental principles, the principles that are constructed by divine and authoritative governance regarding the moral standards and the meanings of human life, indicates that the originally developed systems and ideas of human civilization in the pre-apocalyptic world have been lost after the catastrophic incident.

In her review entitled "On My Bookshelf: Worlds in Despair," Nancy Mairs comments that *The Road* has portrayed a dark vision of humanity (32). However, regardless of the grim prospect of survival in *The Road*, and despite the remark that "language itself is dying and those who speak it will surely be extinct within a very few generations" (Fisher 14), this post-apocalyptic fiction does not merely demonstrate the struggles of life in the state of devastation and elemental entities, but it also forcefully leads readers to reflect on the basis of the establishment of human bonding, the essentials contributing to a meaningful life, and the fragility of moral values as illustrated through the connection between the catastrophic landscape and the human body. Although *"The Road* is perhaps meant to caution the reader of the difficulties of remaining human after the end—with cannibalism as the ultimate failure of humanity" (Curtis 19), McCarthy actually provides the possibility of the re-creation or re-establishment of human bonding and also emphasizes the basis for a meaningful life. Both human bonding and meaning of life are proposed to be based on trust, empathy, and love, and love in particular is considered an intrinsic human quality and a fundamental characteristic of humanity, though it is neither rigid nor unbreakable in face of survival problems, as shown in the presence of cannibals in the novel.

The "brittleness" of human qualities and moral values is shown through the portrayal of the catastrophic environment and the human body in *The Road*. The term "environment" is not only restricted to refer to nature as "environmental criticism's working conception of 'environment' has broadened in recent years from 'natural' to include also the urban, the interweave of 'built' and 'natural' dimensions in every locale, and the interpenetration of the local by the global" (Buell 12). Lawrence Buell demonstrates the inextricable relationship between environment and human, for "the environment-constructed body of environmentality [is] crucial to health or disease, life or death" (23-4). With this definition of the environment, the land and the human body are shown to be profoundly and intimately linked with each other in McCarthy's novel *The Road*. The lack of direction and sense of perplexity which have evolved in that world of "[b]arren, silent, godless" (McCarthy 2) land in *The Road* are demonstrated through the depiction of the encounters, challenges, and dangers confronted by the two protagonists, the man (the father) and the boy (the son), as they travel through the landscape. The interdependence between land and the human body is thus shown in the resemblance between the state of the landscape and the characters' conditions—the barrenness of the land and the exhaustion of the two protagonists, the darkness of the environment and the "blindness" experienced by the people, the turmoil of the land and the confusion of the protagonists' physical location, as well as the "godlessness" of the situation and the immoral practice of cannibalism.

> The post-apocalyptic land in *The Road* is portrayed as infertile and unpromising with [c]harred and limbless trunks of trees stretching away on every side. Ash moving over the road and the sagging hands of blind wire strung from the blackened lightpoles whining thinly in the wind. A burned

house in a clearing and beyond that a reach of meadowlands stark and gray. (McCarthy 6)

The description of the land, filled with "[t]he mummied dead everywhere" (McCarthy 23), adds to the sense of enervation and devastation. From time to time, corpses are seen across the landscape, and many who are found are like those whose "flesh [has] cloven along the bones, the ligaments dried to tug and taut as wires. Shriveled and drawn like latterday bogfolk, their faces of boiled sheeting, the yellowed palings of their teeth" (McCarthy 23). McCarthy purposefully provides a vague and confused depiction of the landscape to be "wood everwhere, dead limbs and branches scattered over the ground" (McCarthy 75), so that the dead human bodies seem to have blended with the post-apocalyptic environment and become part of a dead, spiritless, and disintegrating landscape.

Not only does the disfigurement of the human corpses resemble the damaged landscape, but the dead bodies also weld with the land, thereby increasing the deadliness of the overall atmosphere. Similarly, the lifelessness of the land is paralleled to the state of the characters' frail, ill-formed and malnourished bodies: the man and the boy "are really skinny" (McCarthy 161); the boy has "thin ribs" (McCarthy 123); the man "seem[s] to have no chin" (McCarthy 161); the cannibal is "lean, wiry, rachitic" (McCarthy 65); the old man Ely has "[g]rayblue eyes half buried in the thin and sooty creases of his skin" (McCarthy 174) and "seem[s] to wilt" (McCarthy 172); the thief is "[s]crawny, sullen, bearded, filthy" (McCarthy 273). McCarthy focuses in particular on the man: he was "[s]logging to the edge of the road with his back to the child where he stood bent with his hands on his knees, coughing. He raised up and stood with weeping eyes. On the gray snow a fine mist of blood" (McCarthy 30). The continuous coughing of the man is a symbol of a weak body that is challenged in the absence of basic necessities such as food, water, and warmth. The weakness and illness in the human body metaphorically reveal the feeble maintenance of moral values in the face of survival.

As the man and the boy journey across the landscape in order to go to the South, supposedly a place suitable for living, they constantly struggle with the way they should act and react when their lives are at stake, as well as the direction they should take when they are not able to see in the world of darkness. The environment surrounding them is full of grayness and blackness:

> The blackness [the man] woke to on those nights was sightless and impenetrable. A blackness to hurt [people's] ears with listening. Often he had to get up. No sound but the wind in the bare and blackened trees. He

> rose and stood tottering in that cold autistic dark with his arms outheld for
> balance while the vestibular calculations in his skull cranked out their
> reckonings. (McCarthy 14)

The blackness of the environment enveloping the man not only causes him
to lose the visual function of his eyes, but the "autistic dark" also attacks
him aurally in the sense that the "friendless" sound encircling him makes
him feel lonely. The essence of loneliness, which evolves from the
atmosphere and which the man experiences, echoes the solitary fight by a
small group of survivors who are against the immoral deeds such as some
cannibalistic practices in the devastating land. In that "[d]ark and black
and trackless" (McCarthy 215) world, the man

> got the binoculars out of the cart and stood in the road and glassed the
> plain down there where the shape of a city stood in the grayness like a
> charcoal drawing sketched across the waste. Nothing to see. (McCarthy 7)

The man and the boy attempt to locate themselves in the darkness;
however, the failure in fixing the location through visual means represents
the threat on the spatial order, and hence, signifies the "moral void that is
encoded in terms of blackness and blindness" (Warde 4). This kind of
vainness in searching for a moral direction and standard is also expressed
when the man unceasingly looks up to the starless sky, having the sky
associated with religious divinity from which most of the moral rules are
derived: "He looked at the sky. A single gray flake sifting down. He
caught it in his hand and watched it expire there like the last host of
christendom" (McCarthy 15). In the pre-apocalyptic world, people might
be able to get some information concerning the time and the season by
looking up to the sky, and observing the climate and the environment;
however, in the post-apocalyptic world, it becomes "[i]mpossible to tell
what time of the day [the man] was looking at" (McCarthy 164) and the
man cannot even provide an answer to the questions: "What time of year?
What age the child?" (McCarthy 279). Therefore, the man's action of
looking up to the sky for any information regarding certain (moral)
guidance and direction appears to be useless and senseless. The
"blindness" of the protagonists in that world is by definition a challenge to
their vision, and thus blurs their ongoing direction and the basis of their
behavior in the state of disorder, chaos, and possible savagery.

Not only does the vainness in mapping the post-apocalytic space with
the visual sensory organs show that the original order in the land has
vanished, but the protagonists' pointlessness in locating themselves by
referring to "the limp and rotting pages" (McCarthy 209) of the map also
indicates a disillusionment about the artificial rational order created in

society. Likewise, "the post-apocalyptic environment in *The Road* foregrounds a larger social order in crisis" (Kollin 158). The map, which is "a potent figure of the postmodern order of simulacra, images without depth, dimension or reference" (Warde 5), is an emblem of spatial construction by humans according to rational reasoning as well as a human's realization and acknowledgement of their places in the world. The man and the boy from time to time take out "[t]he tattered oilcompany roadmap [that] had once been taped together but now it was just sorted into leaves and numbered with crayon in the corners for their assembly" (McCarthy 43) in order to determine their location and future direction. This act of reference to the map is expressed in *Justice, Nature, and the Geography of Difference* as some "critical examinations of the relation to nature [environment which] are simultaneously critical examinations of society" (Harvey 174). Nevertheless, although a map, like a telephone directory, represents order in the pre-apocalyptic society, the map as well as the environment are tattered and no longer carry out this function in the post-apocalyptic world. As a result, the man seems lost and has "no idea what direction they might have taken" (McCarthy 122). Since the social system, rational man-made order, and spatial order before the disaster is replaced by an unsystematic and ungoverned, chaotic state of living after the catastrophe, the reliance on law and order in the spatially and socially disordered post-apocalyptic world is of no avail.

Actually, in *The Road*, the cartographic map, the human-created calendar, the telephone directory and "[t]he names of the towns or the rivers" (McCarthy 216) which represent the social order and position are merely artificial human constructs that are then entirely destroyed in the post-apocalyptic world. This echoes Curtis's claim that "[m]odern political philosophers, who wanted to question the legitimacy of the State as an idea[,] used the state of nature to claim that the State was a human construct and is not natural. Thus government was framed as an artificial construction…" (9). The spatial disorder of the world where the man is not able to locate himself coheres with the pulverization of ethics. The man's forceful questioning of the presence of God, which also symbolically represents the human restraints accorded by authoritative powers, precisely points to the lack of moral supervision previously imposed upon society in the post-apocalyptic world: "Are you there? he whispered. Will I see you at the last? Have you a neck by which to throttle you? Have you a heart? Damn you eternally have you a soul? Oh God, he whispered. Oh God" (McCarthy 10). The act of seeing "god" by means of his eyes is again contested in the "godless" land, given the lack of morality. The absence of divine and human governance in the post-apocalyptic land is portrayed as the situation of "godlessness" in the sense that human behavior is no longer governed or constrained by any external authoritative forces. This consequently leads to the probable loss of moral values as revealed in the case of the cannibals.

When survival is threatened, people's moral constraints loosen up and break down because resources and food are extremely limited while the laws, rules, and systems are entirely destroyed in the post-apocalyptic world as portrayed in *The Road*. The proclamation of the man that "[o]n this road there are no godspoke men" (McCarthy 32) demonstrates the disappearance of moral guidance in the land, and thus leads to the practice of cannibalism depicted in several of the encounters during the pair's journey throughout the landscape. At one point the man and the boy discover a house where there are some "naked people, male and female, all trying to hide, shielding their faces with their hands. On the mattress lay a man with his legs gone to the hip and the stumps of them blackened and burnt" (McCarthy 116); later, the man and the boy "heard hideous shrieks coming from the house" (McCarthy 121), and it is believed that these naked people are killed and eaten by the cannibals. The protagonists know the existence of cannibals in that world and occasionally "passed a metal trashdump where someone had once tried to burn bodies. The charred meat and bones under the damp ash might have been anonymous save for the shapes of the skulls" (McCarthy 159). Although McCarthy does not provide explicit scenes of cannibalism, the murky descriptions of these occasions encountered by the protagonists sufficiently reveal this immoral practice in the post-apocalyptic world. From these instances of cannibalism, *The Road* successfully evokes a lamentation over the deplorable loss and disappearance of morality when laws, rules, and governance become absent.

The practice of cannibalism in *The Road* is merely one of the various examples that showcases the sides of weakness, savagery and immorality in humans when life itself is at stake. McCarthy illustrates that the esteemed and revered values and morals held by institutional authorities before the apocalyptic event are easily distorted and broken in the "unrestricted" post-apocalyptic world of "[s]o little of promise" (McCarthy 92). This "little... promise" is doubly interpreted in the sense that, firstly, the prospect of future living in that world is not very positive due to the lack of resources such as food and water, and secondly, the guidelines and standards defining good (moral) behavior in that world are warped and have nearly perished. The vanishing of moral behavior is not only obvious in the cannibals' actions, but is even gradually observed in the behavior of one of the protagonists—the man's questionable conduct. The man always makes promises to the boy, yet fails to fulfill his promises; for instance, the boy proclaims that he must "watch [his father] all the time" (McCarthy 35) in order to prevent him from breaking his promises. Besides, the man promises the boy that he will not leave the boy (McCarthy 119), and he "will not send [the boy] into the darkness alone" (McCarthy 265); yet he is not able to keep his word when he is dying at the end and "cant hold [his] son dead in [his] arms" (McCarthy 298). There is even an occasion in which the man tries to persuade the boy that the house is not dangerous, even though he is not sure about the conditions inside the house and the possible consequences of entering it (McCarthy 217). Failing to keep promises is therefore construed as an act of lying. Hence, the future of developing a larger community in that world is not considered as bright not only because there are little resources supplied by the land for life maintenance and sustenance of the physical body, but also because there is little practice and exertion of moral behavior, fundamental and influential to a meaningful life.

A significant issue concerning the fungibility or alterability of moral values is thus raised: Should moral values be altered according to or depending on different situations? The answer is a "no," that morality should not be contingent upon situations or one's position as depicted in *The Road*. There are several occasions when the man tries to justify and rationalize his actions. For example, he justifies not helping other people, and taking other people's property and causing harm to them. The man and the boy come across a man who has "been struck by lightning" (McCarthy 51) and "was as burntlooking as the country, his clothing scorched and black. One of his eyes was burnt shut and his hair was but a nitty wig of ash upon his blackened skull" (McCarthy 51). Encountering this helpless, "burntlooking" man, the boy very much wants to offer help to him and tries to urge his father to help the dying man; however, his father claims that "[t]here's nothing to be done for [that dying man]" (McCarthy 51) because "[h]e's going to die. [They] cant share what [they] have or [they will] die too" (McCarthy 53). In addition, the man discovers some resources such as food and clothing across the landscape, asserting that the owners "[are] probably dead" (McCarthy 259) even when he is not sure, so that the man and the boy can comfort themselves that they "[are] not taking their stuff" (McCarthy 259), and thus they are not taking or stealing others' property. The man is trying to justify his actions so that he can rely on his set of rules and guidelines that are based on his hypothesized inference.

A similar kind of justification is also found when the man forces a thief to "[t]ake [his] clothes off" (McCarthy 274) as well as to give his shoes up even after the thief has returned the cart with all their food and blankets to them. This causes the thief to be "[s]tanding there raw and naked, filthy, starving. Covering himself with his hand. He was already shivering" (McCarthy 275). Although at first it is the thief who steals the man's and the boy's possessions, the man's self-defense and kind of retaliatory action is morally equivalent to what the thief has done. In this instance, the boy is reluctant to hurt the thief and implores his father not to harm the thief, yet the man justifies his actions by claiming that "[the thief is] going to die anyway" (McCarthy 277). Nevertheless, just as the boy has mentioned, "[i]f you break little promises you'll break big ones" (McCarthy 34-5), Erik J. Wielenberg argues in his article "God, Morality, and Meaning in Cormac McCarthy's *The Road*" that "the man's actions may be justified. But there is a danger lurking here. The danger is that engaging in justified violations of the code of the good guys can make unjustified violations more likely; a slippery slope lurks" (5). This shows that there is a risk of violating and contradicting other rules and values if the violation of some seemingly "minor" values is justified and rationalized.

Nonetheless, regardless of the possible doom and gloom future in the post-apocalyptic world of the novel, McCarthy enables readers to realize the importance of love in human behavior under grim situations and struggles. The boy is always the one who initiates help and shows love for others, including the little boy, the dog, the old man Ely, and the thief. Even after the boy has experienced a menace to his life when meeting the bad guy who threatened to kill him, the boy does not change his will to take care of others and continues to offer help to people he encounters along the road. The boy's uninterrupted good deeds in helping others signify the presence of his inherent and inborn goodness which plays an important role in developing human bonding. As a result, "[o]nly a good guy who has the ability to make connections with other people, to enter or help form a community, truly carries the fire" (Wielenberg 8). Fire, which literally gives warmth to people, is metaphorically a symbol in the novel for making life meaningful. The man and the boy always need to look for some materials that can keep them warm along their journey; this act also parallels the hope for meeting the good guys along the road. The boy is the one who is able to connect with other people and who genuinely carries the fire that symbolizes and underlies human civilization.

Contrary to Wielenberg, who proposes that "[p]ersons [unlike tools,] have an intrinsic worth that must always be valued and respected" (4), the cannibals as depicted in *The Road* have lost and lack this intrinsic worth since they classify humans as mere tools and instruments by assigning people different functions: "slaves [for performing hard toil]...... the women [for exercising sexual needs and reproducing babies as food], perhaps a dozen in number, some of them pregnant, and lastly a supplementary consort of catamites [for entertainment] illclothed against the cold and fitted in dogcollars and yoked each to each" (McCarthy 96). As a result, everyone in the post-apocalyptic world is afraid of the cannibals and tries to avoid getting in touch with them so that the cannibals do not form any bonds with others and are isolated from other people. In the event that everyone acts like the cannibals who treat human bodies as mere tools without intrinsic human worth, humanity, including human bonding and the meaning of life, will gradually become extinct. In fact, McCarthy argues that the intrinsic human value that contributes meaning to life is the quality of love. Love, which is obviously demonstrated through the relationship between the man and the boy in the novel, is the basis for empathy and trust that are important to the establishment of human bonding and the granting of meaning in life: the man shows his paternal love to the boy while the boy displays his love to his father through the sharing of food and water (McCarthy 23) so that a strong and firm bonding, which assists in sustaining the man's life, is created between them.

On the other hand, the mother, who has committed suicide, reveals the importance of love, as well as trust, in the establishment of human bonding. The mother seems to have lost hope in that world in the sense that she no longer possesses trust in anyone in the unpromising post-apocalyptic world. She does not even trust the man, her husband, because he reveals that "[h]er cries [on the day the boy was born] meant nothing to him" (McCarthy 61). The bond between the mother and the father broke since then. When the mother has decided to commit suicide, she remarked that

> [t]hey say that women dream of danger to those in their care and men of danger to themselves. But I dont dream at all… My heart was ripped out of me the night he [the boy] was born… The one thing I can tell you is that you wont survive for yourself. (McCarthy 59)

It turns out the mother did not care for anyone anymore. Her linkage with the family is disconnected due to her lack of trust in the man and her loss of faith in that world. The mother resolutely states that

> [a] person who had no one would be well advised to cobble together some passable ghost. Breathe it into being and coax it along with words of love. Offer it each phantom crumb and shield it from harm with your body. (McCarthy 59)

This statement shows that she prefers not to protect her physical body, remain in a land without morality, and preserve her life with unethical practices; rather, her "only hope is for eternal nothingness" (McCarthy 59) and so she chooses to commit suicide instead of living with no love, no (spiritual) connection and linkage with anyone. The mother precisely demonstrates that the lack of human connection as a result of the absence of love and trust will lead to the lack of meaning in sustaining one's life.

Burkard Sievers asserts in his article, "Against All Reason: Trusting in Trust," that trusting others refers to the feeling of safety and security in relying and depending on them, and this feeling contributes to the connection among people (31), while David P. Levine explains the quality of empathy in his book *The Capacity for Civic Engagement: Public and Private Worlds of the Self*:

> To exercise the capacity for empathy, we must suspend what we would otherwise presume to know about others based on the assumption that they must be the same as us. Empathy begins when we enter into the mental state of another person. This is done, however, in a way that acknowledges the other's experience is not our own but something separate and distinct from it. While empathy begins when we enter into the other's mental state, it requires an additional and distinct connection, which is the connection we refer to as understanding. (78-9)

Therefore, losing the intimately related qualities of trust and empathy, which are significant and indispensable for the development of human connection and bonding, leads to insecurity in the human body in the land of no authoritative protection against immoral deeds. Along the journey, the man is shown to be extremely cautious. Although the man instructs the boy insistently "to keep going" (McCarthy 297), when he is going to die and leave the child, he warns the child to "[k]eep the gun with [him] at all times. [The man asks the boy] to find the good guys but [warns the boy that the boy] cant take any chances" (McCarthy 297-8). This displays the man's inability to trust others and enlarge his social circle; instead, the boy is his "world entire" (McCarthy 4). As Donovan Gwinner posits, "[I]t is as if the father must die for the boy to find what the father is seemingly unprepared to find: good guys, namely the veteran and his family" (153). Unlike the father, the boy possesses the ability to connect with other people, and he is always willing to help others, and as such, he embodies the fundamental human qualities of empathy, trust, and love within himself. Without following his father's instruction, the boy "take[s] a shot" (McCarthy 303) and "[hands the veteran] the pistol" (McCarthy 305); this shows that the boy is able to get along with the veteran's family at the end of the novel, and possibly rebuild the human bonding with different people along the road, thus reestablishing a new community.

Trust is shown to be indispensable in the establishment of a human connection that contributes to the meaning of life. Similarly, "[t]he absence of connections with others is the real threat to meaning and value; the source of meaning and value is love" (Wielenberg 11). One of the man's memories about the past that shows a day he spent with his uncle in the countryside is described as "the perfect day of his childhood. This the day to shape the days upon" (McCarthy 12). Even though "[n]either [the man nor his uncle] had spoken a word" (McCarthy 12), it is exactly the intimate interaction and profound connection shared between them that contributes to the "perfection" of the day, and hence the meaning of life. The human body and the land are intensely attached to, dependent on, and entangled with each other in the sense that humans shape the atmosphere and the form of the land while the land affects human actions as well as the development of the body. On this basis, McCarthy, through the depiction of the frailness of the human body in the "godless" land of delicacy, criticizes the fragility of human intrinsic values, such as empathy, trust, and love toward each other, as well as the alterability of moral values. Nevertheless, despite the fact that no one can provide an absolute answer to the question: "Could there be anything else at the end of the road/*The Road*?" (Gwinner 156), if the chance to survive in such a devastating world is uncertain, McCarthy does not deny the possibility of "rekindling" moral behaviors and reshaping human civilization in that post-apocalyptic world lacking human and divine governance. Similarly, Levine sheds light on the optimistic side of forging human connections:

> To accept that the world is ruled by an evil power is to give up any hope for love, whereas to protect the goodness of the family by taking on its badness keeps hope alive. That is, if we can—through good works, for example—redeem ourselves, we will once again become worthy of love. But doing so is of no use if there is no good object in the world to provide the love we seek. (73)

Therefore, McCarthy's novel *The Road* contends that the idea that people should act as the good guys under the belief that "the fire" will never be extinguished is exactly the necessity in life.

Works Cited

Buell, Lawrence. *The Future of Environmental Criticism: Environmental Crisis and Literary Imagination*. Malden, MA: Blackwell Publishers, 2005. Print.

Curtis, Claire P. *Post-apocalyptic Fiction and the Social Contract*. Lanham, MD: Lexington Books, 2010. Print.

Fisher, Mark. "The Lonely Road." *Film Quarterly* 63.3 (2010): 14-17. Web. 10 Dec. 2012.

Gwinner, Donovan. "'Everything uncoupled from its shoring': Quandaries of Epistemology and Ethics in *The Road*." *Cormac McCarthy: All the Pretty Horses, No Country for Old Men, The Road*. Ed. Sara L. Spurgeon. London; NY: Continuum International Publishing Group, 2011. Print.

Harvey, David. *Justice, Nature and the Geography of Difference*. Cambridge, Mass.: Blackwell Publishers, 1996. Print.

Kollin, Susan. "'Barren, silent, godless': Ecodisaster and the Post-abundant Landscape in *The Road*." *Cormac McCarthy: All the Pretty Horses, No Country for Old Men, The Road*. Ed. Sara L. Spurgeon. London; NY: Continuum International Publishing Group, 2011. Print.

Levine, David P. *The Capacity for Civic Engagement: Public and Private Worlds of the Self*. NY: Palgrave Macmillan, 2011. Print.

Mairs, Nancy. Rev. of *Oryx and Crake*, by Margaret Atwood, and *The Road*, by Cormac McCarthy. *The Women's Review of Books* 24.2 (2007): 32. Web. 10 Dec. 2012.

McCarthy, Cormac. *The Road*. London: Picador, 2010. Print.

Sievers, Burkard. "Against All Reason: Trusting in Trust." *Organizational & Social Dynamics* 3.1 (2003): 19-39. Print.

Warde, Anthony "'Justified in the World': Spatial Values and Sensuous Geographies in Cormac McCarthy's *The Road*." *University of Edinburgh Postgraduate Journal of Culture & the Arts* Spring (2010): n. pag. Web. 6 Apr. 2012.

Wielenberg, Erik J. "God, Morality, and Meaning in Cormac McCarthy's *The Road*." *Cormac McCarthy Journal* 8.1 (2010): 1-16. Web. 7 Apr. 2012.

CHAPTER SIX

BODIES OF DEBT:
INTERROGATING THE COSTS
OF TECHNOLOGICAL PROGRESS, SCIENTIFIC
ADVANCEMENT, AND SOCIAL CONQUESTS
THROUGH DYSTOPIAN LITERATURE

MELISSA AMES

The Umbrella Concept: Using Dystopian Texts to Promote Social Responsibility

Educational institutes have long been associated with the role of teaching social responsibility. By definition, social responsibility is "a personal investment in the well-being of people and the planet" (Berman 15). However, despite the fact that many feel that public schools and universities are ideal sites for this type of training, research has found that many instructors are reluctant to discuss controversial issues within their classrooms because of the potential negative ramifications. A recent study found that only "11% of students reported spending time in their classes on 'problems facing the country today'" (Wolk 667). Further research has found that such issues "receive little attention in schools because in the culture of schooling, and the culture of society, many controversial topics and issues are taboo" (Evans, Avery, and Pederson 295). These cultural taboos "impose severe disabilities on teaching and thinking" and ultimately impact the decisions instructors make concerning course content and classroom management (Evans, Avery, and Pederson 295).

When instructors do go against the societal grain and merge such subject matter into their courses, some common issues surface. Brian K. Payne and Randy R. Gainey describe two likely scenarios that instructors will be faced with when controversial topics are at the center of classroom discussion: "(a) a small number of students may want to voice their opinions at the expense of excluding other students, or (b) all of the students may simply avoid eye contact and hope the professor will not make them talk about their ideas" (55). To further complicate the situation, other factors can also impact how likely a class is to engage in critical thinking practices surrounding social topics. Payne and Gainey explain that various "gender and demographic differences" may "affect an individual's beliefs and attitudes toward many controversial issues," as well as their willingness to openly discuss their views (55).

Despite these difficulties, studies have found that there are numerous benefits to crafting a course that forces students to engage in such critical inquiry. Research finds that the study of controversial topics, if discussed within an open and supportive classroom environment, promotes "increased political interest and civic tolerance and decreased dogmatism" (Evans, Avery, and Pederson 297). In "Teaching Supercharged Subjects," David Pace, an Associate Professor in the History Department at Indiana University, discussed a challenging course he taught on "The Dawn of the Atomic Age." Throughout many of his first attempts at teaching this course, he found that students quickly "began to assume uncharacteristically extreme positions, and conflicts within the class threatened to poison interactions for the remainder of the course" (Pace 42). Pace was further troubled by the way the students' unwavering views affected him as a teacher. He writes, "the extreme nature of many students' comments pushed my 'buttons,' and the emotional and intellectual chaos of the argument made me less effective as an agent of critical thinking" (Pace 42). Ultimately he was able to restructure the class so that it produced more favorable results, and he highlights ten strategies that ultimately worked to produce a more productive classroom atmosphere. Some of these strategies include: providing students with the necessary skills to engage with the debate (e.g. analyzing a question from multiple perspectives, supporting an argument with research); setting the foundation for the controversial issue and controlling the instructional pace (e.g. exposing students to a controversial topic slowly and incrementally); and managing the classroom dynamic and conversation (e.g. ensuring the conversation stems from the students but intervening as necessary and making sure that logic rather than emotion motivates arguments) (Pace 43-45). Other best practices for tackling tricky topics within classroom study include creating an inquiry unit where the teacher begins with a question, or set of questions, that connects the various topics of discussion and textual analysis (Wolk 666). This allows the overarching thematic focus of the class, more so than the individual topics of conflict, to be the foundation to build upon. This umbrella places various debates in dialogue with one another and broadens the conversation, while it also helps to prevent students from disengaging if one specific topic is not appealing to them. Another crucial component to crafting a successful course that encourages social responsibility is text selection. Payne and Gainey encourage instructors to select texts that engage students in critical thinking about social issues because they provide a specific context in which to explore a larger social critique (57). This is where fictional narratives – particularly those entrenched in the utopian and dystopian tradition – can be extremely useful.

Discussing novels in particular, Carrie Hintz and Elaine Ostry argue that dystopian literature "encourages people to view their society with a critical eye, sensitizing or predisposing them to political action" (7). They suggest that "exposure to these types of texts can lead young readers to see inequality in their own communities and countries" (Hintz and Ostry 8). Scholars such as Jacqueline N. Glasglow encourage utilizing dystopian novels in social justice units, arguing that "social justice education has the potential to prepare citizens who are sophisticated in their understanding of diversity and group interaction, able to critically evaluate social institutions, and committed to working democratically with diverse others" (Glasglow 54). Similarly, Steven Wolk believes that reading dystopian novels allows "students to question the world we have and envision a better world we could have" because these texts "offer unique opportunities to teach these habits of mind" (668). Although these stories are often set in the future, usually in post-apocalyptic settings, Wolk argues that "thematically they are really about the present" (668).

This essay discusses the successes and challenges of teaching a particular cross-curricular course that focused on controversial issues appearing in scientific research and dystopian literature. The course studied narratives that wrestle with ethical concerns surrounding "progress" (societal achievements, technological advancement, scientific discoveries, and so forth). Contemporary debates and specific issues addressed throughout this course included cloning, stem cell research, black market organ transplants, human trafficking, surveillance technology, euthanasia, and capital punishment. In alignment with research concerning best practices in teaching social responsibility topics, this course was centered on a set of inquiry questions that stretched across all units, texts, and discussions. It also utilized narratives as the site of inquiry – as the safe space in which to wrestle with these controversial issues. In this class students analyzed various fictional dysopian texts (novels, film, and television) that critique the above-mentioned issues, and class discussion revolved around the following questions: what do we do when human survival and societal progress come at extreme costs, and how might such advancements question our faith in humanity? The theme of indebted bodies – bodies created by technology, dependent on technology, governed by technology, or punished by technology – was present in all of the literary and media texts students covered. This motif was studied in the following novels and short stories: Brian Aldiss's "Super Toys," MT Anderson's *Feed*, Isaac Asimov's *I, Robot*, Margaret Atwood's *The Handmaid's Tale*, Philip K. Dick's "Minority Report," Cory Doctorow's *Little Brother*, Aldous Huxley's *Brave New World*, Kazuo Ishiguro's *Never Let Me Go*, and Scott Westerfeld's *Uglies*, as well as in contemporary film companion texts, such as *A.I. Artificial Intelligence, I, Robot, Minority Report, The Life of David Gayle, The Island*, and *Repo Men*.

The Student Body: Understanding Course Objectives and Desired Outcomes

This course was designed as a general education literature class for undergraduate students. The normal composition of such a class is 20-25 students, primarily non-English majors of sophomore or junior status. The course objectives were designed so that by the end of the semester students would be able to demonstrate the following skills:

1. Read fiction and nonfiction texts that exhibit a wide range of cultural perspectives and values, and develop abilities to think critically and write analytically about them.
2. Engage in reading and writing experiences about literature in order to demonstrate an increased understanding or an appreciation for social, cultural, intellectual, and aesthetic ideas and their discovery.
3. Develop research skills, including effective use of source materials and the principles of documentation, and apply those skills to the study of literature and media analysis.
4. Understand the relationship that narratives have to one another (despite differences in media or genre) and to the cultural/social/ historical milieu in which they are created, produced, and consumed.
5. Analyze thematic variations across media and genre in order to determine the effects of narrative format.
6. Apply research from outside disciplines (e.g. science, law, ethics) to the study of literature, film, television, and other artifacts from popular culture.

7. Work collaboratively in order to explore ideas, formulate arguments, and present findings in a scholarly fashion.

While these were the objectives articulated on the syllabus, the course also aimed to teach social responsibility– an outcome not as easily measured as those listed above.

Dissecting a Course Design: Applying Literary Studies to Science, Law, and Medicine

This course was divided into three thematic units: 1) Exploring the Consequences of Technological Progress; 2) Critiquing the Changing Justice System; and 3) Ethical Debates within Science and Medicine. Each unit was further divided into sub-units focused on specific technological advances or instances of human progress. These sub-units contained textual sets where students analyzed the topic of focus within a literary work, film, and various non-fiction texts from contemporary discourse.

Exploring the Consequences of Technological Progress

As the first unit of the semester, which established the overarching focus of the course and helped to build crucial student skills, this was the longest. This seven-week unit focused on a variety of sub-units that were in dialogue with one another. Students began the course with a sub-unit critiquing human dependence on technology. They began by reading scholarly critiques of the digital generation – Nicholas Carr's "Is Google Making Us Stupid?" and Mark Bauerlein's *The Dumbest Generation*. These non-fiction articles functioned as preliminary readings for M.T. Anderson's *Feed*, a novel that explores (and exaggerates) these scholars' very concerns. *Feed*, a young adult dystopian novel, is set in the future, and showcases a world completely dependent on technology. The most prominent example of this is "the feed" – a computing chip inserted into the brain that allows one to be constantly connected to a stream of information (an advanced version of our Internet). Throughout the novel, Anderson displays the consequences of this technology (and others), such as the lessening of intelligence and independent thought, highlighted through the constant use of slang, frequent statements of ignorance, and the depiction of educational institutes run solely for corporate profit. This sub-unit required students to research issues such as the effects of social networking on communication and human relations and the consequences of living in a consumerist culture.

Students then shifted into a different, although related, sub-unit on robotics. As in the previous sub-unit, students debated the benefits and detriments of technology, interrogating the question "how far is too far" with reference to technological innovations. In this sub-unit students analyzed two sets of adaptations to see how the various creators carried out their social commentaries differently. Specifically, students read Brian Aldiss's short story, "Super Toys," viewed Steven Spielberg's film *A. I. Artificial Intelligence*, critiqued select short stories from Isaac Asimov's collection *I, Robot*, and then watched Alex Proyas's film adaptation of the same name. Because both Spielberg and Proyas's movies were very loose adaptations of the original literary works, students were prevented from falling into the trap of simply comparing and contrasting the plots of these texts. Yet, despite their different narrative threads, each text delved into the same theme concerning technology. "Super Toys" and *A.I.* focus on the creation of a robotic child programmed to love its human "parents." To varying degrees, these texts delve into the moral question of whether such a creation is humane and what, if any, responsibility humans would then have to love their adopted robots in return. Both the print and film versions of *I, Robot*, explore different consequences of a world reliant on robotic technology – specifically the potential for technology to evolve beyond humans' control. In conjunction with this sub-unit, students researched existing technologies, such as current attempts to achieve artificial intelligence, and analyzed the implications these technologies might have on human civilization.

The third sub-unit focused on technology's ability to manipulate and control human bodies. In this section, students studied one young adult novel and one canonical novel, each of which inquires into this issue in different ways. In Scott Westerfeld's *Uglies* (the first of his four-part young adult series), readers are presented with a post-apocalyptic world in which all human problems have seemingly been erased. As is the typical dystopian formula, this world is depicted as a utopia before its dark underside is revealed. In this society, all persons undergo an operation at the age of sixteen that turns them "pretty" – erasing all physical imperfections and eliminating the issues the previous era had with racial inequality or unfair competitions based on cultural beauty standards. Unbeknownst to the citizens who undergo this procedure, they also obtain lesions on their brains that alter their ability to think critically (which, ultimately, is the reason there are no longer conflicts; it is not the even playing field of biological beauty that has erased all confrontation but the inability to hold divergent views and independent thoughts). In this portion of the sub-unit, students researched the consequences of media imagery and current trends concerning cosmetic procedures in order to discuss how this text critiques contemporary societal beauty standards.

The next novel students studied was Aldous Huxley's *Brave New World,* which depicts the body not simply altered by technology, but the body as created by technology – more specifically, advanced reproductive technology. Huxley crafts a world in which humans are designed and reared into various caste systems, receiving physical and mental traits based on their social hierarchy and utility, as well as various privileges linked to their social standing. Like many of the texts studied in this first large unit, the society depicted in this novel strategically controls its population through distraction. (Some examples within the novel include required recreational sex and mandatory drug use). Together, *Brave New World* and *Uglies* allow students to question the potential consequences that could accompany a government's strategic use of technological advancements.

Critiquing the Changing Justice System

The second half of the semester contained two shorter – and more narrowly focused – units. The first unit explored the ways in which bodies are monitored, controlled, and punished under the current justice system. Students read Philip K. Dick's short story, "The Minority Report," and viewed Steven Spielberg's film adaptation. The shared narrative features a futuristic world in which a pre-crime unit is in place; due to its superb functioning, it has eliminated homicide. This pre-crime unit works by exploiting the psychic abilities of three pre-cogs – humans with the ability to predict with relative accuracy the homicidal impulses of humans. Studying these texts allowed students to continue to address issues such as bodily exploitation (through the treatment of the pre-cogs), at the same time that they interrogated the justice system as a whole, especially one that becomes increasingly more dependent on technology to locate and punish criminals. From this textual set, students moved to two works that evoke contemporary debates concerning the justice system. Corey Doctorow's post-9/11 young adult novel, *Little Brother,* is an obvious critique of the United States Patriot Act. Students read this novel, viewed selected clips from Tony Scott's (pre-9/11) film, *Enemy of the State,* and researched the Patriot Act in order to debate issues such as privacy rights, governmental surveillance procedures, and homeland security.

The second contemporary debate students were involved in during this unit surrounds capital punishment. This well-trodden controversial topic is explored through student research along with Alan Parker's film, *The Life of David Gale*. Parker's movie follows the trial of a man wrongfully accused of murder and his resulting death sentence. The film concludes with viewers realizing that the victim had actually committed suicide because she was facing a terminal illness. The two collaborated in her "assisted suicide," knowing full well that he would likely be tried for murder. As opponents of the death penalty, they were hoping that this case would prove its fallibility. Following this film, students presented research on the contemporary debates surrounding both capital punishment and euthanasia (or, specifically, physician-assisted suicide).

Ethical Debates within Science and Medicine

The final unit of the course is by far the most eclectic of all, housing debates central to science and medicine, as well as religion and politics. Beginning with the former, students read Kazuo Ishiguro's novel, *Never Let Me Go*, and viewed Michael Bay's *The Island*, in order to enter into contemporary debates about the ethics of cloning. Students researched this specific issue and other related medical debates, such as those surrounding stem cell research. Students then moved on to study advanced reproductive technology and sexual exploitation. The class read Margaret Atwood's *The Handmaid's Tale*, which features a main character living under the futuristic totalitarian Christian theocracy that has replaced the United States government. Her role is that of a concubine (a "handmaid") kept for reproductive purposes within the household of a ruling class family who suffers, as does the society at large, from fertility problems. In perhaps the greatest narrative reach of the semester, this novel is then connected to current global atrocities such as human sex trafficking. Continuing on with the focus of the exploited body, students viewed Miguel Sapochnik's *Repo Men*, a film which portrays a futuristic world in which corporations take advantage of the ill, allowing people to buy artificial organs on credit. Students then related real world issues concerning black market organ sales.

Textual Connections: Developing the Skill Synthesize Social Critiques

One of the primary goals of this literature class was to make textual associations, primarily in the form of text-to-text and text-to world connections. Quite obviously, the units and sub-units prompted students to analyze various related storylines – texts that shared some basic narrative thread (content) or social critique (theme). However, it also turned out to be very important for students to make connections between texts studied in different portions of the class. The following is an example of three overarching issues dealt with during the course, and some textual analysis of the works that highlighted them.

The Consequences of Advanced Technology

One theme that students studied pertained to the consequences of advanced technology. In their early readings, they were forced to entertain the arguments of academics who specifically critique their generation's dependency on technology.

> We have entered the Information Age, traveled down the Information Superhighway, spawned a Knowledge Economy, undergone the Digital Revolution, converted manual workers into knowledge workers, and promoted a Creative Class, and we anticipate a Conceptual Age to be... And yet, while teens and young adults have absorbed digital tools into their daily lives like no other age group, while they have grown up with more knowledge and information readily at hand, taken more classes, built their own Web sites, enjoyed more libraries, bookstores, and museums in their towns and cities... in sum, while the world has provided them extraordinary chances to gain knowledge and improve their reading/writing skills, not to mention offering financial incentives to do so, young Americans today are no more learned or skillful than their predecessors, no more knowledgeable, fluent, up-to-date, or inquisitive, except in the materials of youth culture. (Baurelein 8-9)

Baurelein forcefully argues: "all the ingredients are in place for making an informed and intelligent citizen – but it's not happening" (10). He laments the current societal conditions: "instead of opening young American minds to the stores of civilization and science and politics, technology has contracted their horizon to themselves, to the social scene around them. Young people have never been so intensely mindful of and present to one another, so enabled in adolescent contact" (Baurelein 10). Baurelein's criticisms align well with the social commentary provided in *Feed*. After only hours of being disconnected from the feed, the main character, Titus, begins complaining about its disappearance through an interior monologue that showcases just how crucial he and his peers feel this technological apparatus is to their daily existence:

> I missed the feed. I don't know when they first had feeds. Like maybe, fifty or a hundred years ago. Before that, they had to use their hands and their eyes. Computers were all outside the body. They carried them around

outside of them, in their hands, like if you carried your lungs in a briefcase
and opened it to breathe. (Anderson 47)

In this course students were trained to study not only the actual content of
the narratives but their form as well. Both Anderson's *Feed* and
Westerfeld's *Uglies* perform their social commentary about the negative
effects of technology through various formal techniques. Both authors
draw upon informal diction (the use of slang and improper syntax) to
highlight the ignorance of the characters within their novels.

Meanwhile, other texts studied throughout the term focus more on the
potentially detrimental effects technology could have on human relations
rather than intellect. In "Super Toys," Aldiss includes the speech of a CEO
promoting the launch of his newest robotic creation: a serving-man, which
he promised would help millions who suffer from increased loneliness and
isolation. The serving-man will increase their quality of life because "he
will always answer, and the most vapid conversation cannot bore him…
personal isolation will then be banished (Aldiss 198).

In a slightly different focus, the various short stories from *I, Robot*, as
well as "Super Toys," *A.I. Artificial Intelligence*, and the film adaptation
of *I, Robot*, tackle the moral question of whether we should want to create
emotional bonds between humans and robots. Spielberg's *A.I.*, addresses
this issue by aligning viewers' sympathies with the main character, David,
a robotic boy. Throughout the film David seeks to secure the love of his
human adopted mother, not understanding that doing so is a near
impossibility. In a telling scene, a fellow robot tries to demonstrate to
David why this love is unattainable:

> She loves what you do for her… but she does not love you… she cannot
> love you. You are neither flesh, nor blood. You are not a dog, a cat, or a
> canary. You were designed and built specific, like the rest of us. And you
> are alone now only because they tired of you, or replaced you with a
> younger model, or were displeased with something you said, or broke.
> They made us too smart, too quick, and too many. We are suffering for the
> mistakes they made because when the end comes, all that will be left is us.
> That's why they hate us. (*A.I*)

The closing lines of this speech speak to another motif surfacing in many
of the texts: to what extent would humans go if they felt their security or
their very existence was threatened by their technological creations?
Although most of the narratives studied in class showcased worlds in
which people have embraced and become dependent on technology, some
texts also included moments in which we see subgroups who protest
against the technological advances. *A.I.* features a graphic scene where

humans torture robots at a "Flesh Fair"; *I, Robot* portrays a main character, Detective Del Spooner (Will Smith), who is accused of robot bigotry; and Asimov's short story collection includes extended commentary about the fears and biases against robots – specifically through the discussion of the Society for Humanity.

The Effects of Technology on the Environment

Another thematic thread surfacing throughout many of the narratives studied in this course was the effects that technological advancements have on the environment. Although many narratives touch on this theme briefly, the novel that most explicitly does so is Anderson's *Feed*. Throughout the novel the declining state of Earth is shown through depictions of suburbs existing under protective domes; dead seas that can only be visited when wearing protective suits; and discussions of national parks being eliminated in order to build air factories (Anderson 88, 129, 179). Anderson is clearly critiquing human waste at various points in his novel in sometimes comical and sometimes serious ways. One ridiculous scene finds the main character's mother and brother crinkling up "the disposable table" so that it can be thrown away after just one use (Anderson 129). And in a more emotional scene toward the end of the novel, the father of a dying girl makes this enraged speech about the wasteful practices of American citizens: "We Americans are interested only in the consumption of our products. We have no interest in how they were produced, or what happens to them once we discard them, once we throw them away" (Anderson 290).

This theme of waste surfaces in Aldiss's short story as well, in a key moment from the CEO's speech:

> Though three-quarters of the overcrowded world are starving, we are lucky here to have more than enough, thanks to population control. Obesity's our problem, not malnutrition. I guess there's nobody round this table who doesn't have a Crosswell working for him in the small intestine, a perfectly safe tape-worm that enables its host to eat up to fifty per cent more food and still keep his or her figure. Right? (195)

The various films viewed throughout the term show the consequences of human waste as only a visual display can. The most striking of these are the closing scenes of *A.I.*, which depict a destroyed vision of New York City, first in ruins and later under water. The film ends with a scene two thousand years in the future – long past the end of humanity during a time in which aliens reside on Earth and humans cease to exist.

The Costs of Cultural Beauty Standards

A less serious, but perhaps more timely, societal critique surfacing throughout many of these narratives is the effects of the media on society. Westerfeld's series grounds its commentary on the current surge in cosmetic surgery and offers "an impetus for an important dialogue about beauty standards and our culture's" captivation with them (Scott and Dragoo 11). In one scene the main character of *Uglies*, Tally, is flipping through old celebrity magazines from the "Rusty Era" (a period meant to refer to our contemporary times). Her interior monologue demonstrates how drastically she and her contemporaries have been brainwashed into believing that physical differences amount to only imperfections:

> She'd never seen so many wildly different faces before. Mouths and eyes and noses of every imaginable shape, all combined insanely on people of every age. And the bodies. Some were grotesquely fat, or weirdly over muscled, or uncomfortably thin, and almost all of them had wrong, ugly proportions. But instead of being ashamed of their deformities, the people were laughing and kissing and posing, as if all the pictures had been taken at some huge party. (Westerfeld 198)

This topic is broached in *Feed* also. In this novel Anderson depicts the characters as being mindless trend followers, quickly running off to change their hairstyles or self-mutilate their bodies if the current fashion trend demands it. In an interview with James Blasingame, Anderson notes that, in addition to serving as a cautionary tale about the misuse of technology, his novel was intended to scrutinize the current culture of instant gratification, aspects of herd psychology, and individuals' refusal to tackle serious societal problems (4).

Cross-Curricular Connections: A Sampling of Assignments & Assessments

Textual connections are at the center of this course's focus, and the assessments in this class strived to show mastery of these as well as traditional literary analysis, research, and writing skills. These assessments also intended to demonstrate the critical thinking skills necessary for academic accomplishments across disciplines. Students completed four primary assignments and two exams throughout this 15-week course. The first two assignments are the most "traditional," while the other two highlight an attention to genre and interdisciplinary boundary blurring not always found in an introductory literature class.

Response Journal

Students completed this ongoing project throughout the semester in order to document their careful reading and literary analysis, as well as their attentive viewing of in-class films. The goal of this collection of essays was to assist them in completing other course work (essays/projects) and to help them prepare for their exams (midterm/final). Therefore, students were asked to craft a 1-2 page entry for each literary work we read and each film we viewed in class. They were encouraged to use these entries during our class discussion when called upon to participate in the analysis of the narrative. These entries were to be formatted according to the requirements listed in the below table.

Format for Literary Responses: For each entry devoted to a print text you should include the following components:

- *Bibliographic Citation* (formatted according to MLA – see OWL Purdue's website for assistance)
- 1-2 paragraph *Summary* of the text (a brief synopsis of the story in *your own words*)
- 1-2 paragraph *Analysis* section (a discussion of the text's importance, overall message, and the social critique implicit within the narrative)
- *Explication* of a key passage or set of related quotes (you should type out a substantial section of the text – an important paragraph – or a few linked quotations and then discuss its/their importance in relation to the text as a whole; you should include the page numbers for these quotations, cited according to MLA with parenthetical citations.)
- *Discussion Questions* (a list of at least 10 questions/issues that you would like to discuss/pose – these can be general questions, but more useful might be questions that point to specific moments in the text that were interesting/confusing; it is suggested that you include potential page numbers to turn to when discussing your question.)

Format for Film Responses: For each entry devoted to a film you should include the following components:

- *Bibliographic Citation* (formatted according to MLA – see OWL Purdue's website for assistance)
- 1-2 paragraph *Summary* of the text (a brief synopsis of the storyline in *your own words*)

- 1-2 paragraph *Analysis* section (a discussion of the text's importance, overall message, and the social critique implicit within the narrative)
- *Explication* of a key scene or set of related scenes (in order to do this you will need to take detailed notes during the viewing experience; you may type out an important moment of dialogue or a few linked quotations and then discuss its/their importance in relation to the text as a whole, or, alternately, you can describe in great detail an important scene focusing on more than just the spoken words, attending to filmic devices (editing, lighting, sound, setting, camera angles, special effects), discussing the effectiveness or effects of these devices (how they worked on the audience, what they intended to do, how they further the narrative and/or the director's message
- *Discussion Questions* (a list of at least 10 questions/issues that you would like to discuss/pose – these can be general questions, but more useful might be specific moments in the film that were interesting/confusing.)

Fig. 1.1. Criteria for Response Journal Entries

Although these response journals were collected periodically throughout the semester for progress checks and informal feedback, they were ultimately assessed as a whole when they were formally submitted for a grade. Students were then assessed based on the four major skill areas described above (summary, analysis, explication, and questioning) and in three more procedure-orientated categories (language and mechanics; layout and bibliographical citation; and completeness and preparation).

Literary Analysis Essay

The second rather standard assignment given to this class was that of a traditional literary analysis essay. Students were asked to craft a research paper integrating outside source material to formulate an argument concerning how a controversial issue is addressed through various narratives. They were to study how these fictional texts provided a social commentary and/or critique about this issue. They were further directed to tackle the overarching questions posed by the class: 1) what ethical concerns surround the area of "progress" explored in their chosen narratives (societal achievements, technological advancement, scientific discoveries, etc.); 2) what these narratives suggest we do when human survival and societal progress come at extreme costs; and 3) how might such advancements question our faith in humanity? This essay was assigned at midterm in order to ensure that students were mastering the material and the skills of the course. The breadth of this essay (with its overarching topic and analysis of multiple texts) was a nice contrast to the more narrowly focused assignments of the course.

Criterion	Below	Satisfactory	Meets	Exceeds
Content (5, 7, 8, 10)	Topic is not adequately covered. The overall paper strays from the argument at hand, does not provide scholarly analysis or reader interest. Does not address course concerns.	Topic coverage could be improved. The overall argument is discussed but scholarly analysis and interest level could be more developed. Addresses course concerns partially.	Good depth & breadth of coverage. Topic is well discussed in a scholarly, unique, and interesting manner. Some originality in topic. Addresses course concerns.	Excellent depth & breadth of coverage. Topic is explored in a scholarly, enjoyable, creative & interesting fashion. An original and academic paper, addressing course concerns.
Genre/ Media (5, 7, 8, 10)	Does not attempt, or does with multiple problems, to analyze media/genre characteristics.	Rarely attends to, or struggles to explain, the particular characteristics of various media/genre, little analysis in this regard.	Addresses the particular characteristics of various media/genre and shows some ability to analyze them.	Attends to the particular characteristics of various media/genre and showcases the ability to skillfully analyze them.
Compre-hension (5, 7, 8, 10)	Does not demonstrate an understanding of the narratives and sources utilized.	Demonstrates some understanding of the narratives and sources utilized. A few accuracy issues.	Demonstrates good understanding of the narrative texts and sources utilized.	Demonstrates thorough understanding of the texts and sources utilizes.

Research	Problems with basic research. Under length requirements. Most or all sources are questionable. Does not show understanding of controversial issue.	Research meets basic requirements. Some questionable sources. Shows some understanding of controversial issue.	Most sources are scholarly in nature and worthy of study. Shows a good understanding of controversial issue.	All sources are scholarly and worthy of study. Shows thorough understanding of controversial issue.
(5, 7, 8, 10)				
Essay Organi- zation (5, 7, 8, 10)	Does not follow the standard essay pattern organization.	Some slips in the standard organizational essay pattern.	Good organization in the standard essay pattern.	Well-crafted, progressing in the standard essay pattern.
Clarity / Logic (5, 7, 8, 10)	Writer has problems organization information. The ability to form & support arguments is not demonstrated.	Writer has some ability to organize information but falters some with clarity in proving and supporting arguments.	Writer is able to organize information and make clear arguments, most of which are supported by examples from the texts.	Writer is able to efficiently organize information & formulate logical, clear arguments with ample textual support.
Synthesis of Material (5, 7, 8, 10)	Does not demonstrate mastery of synthesis writing. Material unconnected.	Demonstrates the ability to synthesize material to some extent.	Demonstrates the ability to synthesize material with a solid outcome.	Demonstrates the ability to synthesize material efficiently.
Language Usage (5, 7, 8, 10)	Lower-level writing. Overall, simple sentences and basic wording. Problems with basic writing conventions.	Decent writing showcased here. Some variety with wording but simple sentences prevail.	Good overall writing. Well worded with a solid amount of sentence variation.	College-level writing. Excellent word variation and complex sentence structure.

Mechanics (5, 7, 8, 10)	Lack of effort with proofreading. Multiple errors	Problems with proofreading. Some errors present.	Pretty well proofread. A few oversights.	Well proofread. Very few oversights.
MLA (5, 7, 8, 10)	Does not show mastery of MLA format. Multiple errors and misuse.	Some problems with understanding MLA format. Some errors and misuse.	Demonstrates basic mastery of MLA format. A few errors and misuse.	Demonstrates high-level mastery of MLA formats. Very minor errors present.

Fig. 1.2 Scoring Rubric for Literary Analysis Essay

Multi-Genre Research Project

While the literary analysis essay asked students to pair texts, the final assessment of the course, the multi-genre research project, allowed students to focus their study on one text alone. Also, while all of the other formal assignments found students writing in traditional academic genres, this assignment allowed them to create a multimodal composition demonstrating advanced research skills through various writing items and creative pieces. In order to showcase a comprehensive understanding of one selected work/pairing, students created projects that creatively captured the literary work's overall narrative, theme, and social commentary. While a traditional exam or essay could have met the same goals, this allowed students a bit more freedom and flexibility when relaying their understanding and investment in the text. This assignment encouraged students to apply their knowledge of the primary text to a variety of genres (written and visual), thus creating a meta-narrative about the work.

From this description it might appear that students had endless choices when it came to the construction of their final projects; however, this was not actually the case. Students were directed to choose one genre from various categories – categories specifically selected to demonstrate different skills and levels of comprehension. Students were encouraged to select the genre within each category that allowed them to most fully showcase their understanding of the text. In the end, they had crafted seven unique pieces for inclusion in their projects. The table below contains the genre selections and categories they had at their disposal.

A. Newspaper Component: Students will compose an item that would appear in a fictional newspaper published in the hometown/area of the narrative text. This item should conform with the genre in question in terms of content, length, tone, and layout.

CHOOSE *ONE* OPTION FROM BELOW:

Obituary: a brief (1/2 or 1 page) blurb about the death of a character from the narrative. This could take place during the narrative or in some perceived (fictional/extended) future. Relevant details from his/her life should be present.

Letter to the Editor: a 1-2 page (double-spaced) letter taking a stand on an issue that occurred within the text. (Note: this cannot be the same issue explored in the research section below).

Advice Column: a 2-part advice column (from the character seeking advice and the fictional expert responding to it). The content of the entry posed by the narrative's character should pull from the storyline and should fit his/her personality.

Front Page Feature Story: a 2 page (double-spaced) article highlighting a key event that took place in the narrative – something that would be "front page" news. This should be fashioned after a real newspaper and should start with an attention grabbing title, important information up front, and it should address all the important W's (who, what, when, where, and why).

Personal Advertisement: a brief personal (dating) advertisement for one of the characters in the text. This should conform to genre standards/length and should fit the character's disposition.

Other (see instructor for approval)

B. Artistic Analysis Piece: Students will select a literary/cultural artifact that a) is intended to capture the essence of the narrative text (i.e. a book jacket cover) or b) they feel represents/captures the essence of the narrative text (i.e. an unrelated text that they feel aligns well with text of study). This item can be found (but then should be cited properly) or originally crafted. Accompanying this piece should be a 1 paragraph justification of why this artifact does (or does not) fit the narrative of study.

CHOOSE *ONE* OPTION FROM BELOW:

Poetry (found or original)

Music Lyrics (found or original)

Product/Company Advertisement (found or original)

Book Cover/Jacket (original design or written analysis/comparison of two different versions in print)

Movie Poster (original design or analysis of published poster's design)

Other (see instructor for approval)

C. Visual Artistic Application Piece: Students will select a piece of visual art that they feel represents/captures the essence of the narrative text. This item can be found (but then should be cited properly) or originally crafted. Accompanying this piece should be a 1 paragraph justification of why this visual fits the narrative of study.

CHOOSE *ONE* OPTION FROM BELOW:
Photograph (found or original)
Sketch/Drawing (found or original)
Political Cartoon (found or original)
Other (see instructor for approval)

D. Character Insight Piece: Students will craft an item that provides insight into one of the characters from the text. This item will require close reading and a review of the narrative in order to select specific characteristics, behaviors, descriptions, etc. Using direct quotes/paraphrases is suggested.

CHOOSE *ONE* OPTION FROM BELOW:
Journal/Diary Entry: a 1-2 page (single-spaced) entry (or set of entries) from a character's perspective detailing a moment from the narrative from his/her vantage point.
Facebook Page: a mock Facebook page for a character including relevant biographical details, likes, friends, and posts. Some of this material should stem directly from the text but others can be inferred based on his/her personality.
Vanity License Plate: a realistically designed vanity license plate (use proper layout) that would represent the character's personality. Attached to this artistic piece should be a 1 paragraph justification of why this vanity plate fits his/her persona as showcased in the narrative.
Text Message/IM exchange: a 1-2 page (single-spaced) transcript for a text message or IM exchange between two characters. The contents of this narrative must be loosely based on the narrative but embellishments are allowed as long as they fit the characters participating in the conversation.
Other (see instructor for approval)

E. Informational Essay: Students will write in an established genre relevant to book production/review. Proper organization, tone, mechanics, and proofreading are expected.

CHOOSE *ONE* OPTION FROM BELOW:

Book Review: a 1-2 page (double-spaced) evaluation essay written in the form of a book review that might be published in a newspaper, magazine, or website. Although some summary will be present, this should be balanced against critique and commentary. Be careful not to be "spoiler" heavy for the audience's sake.

Back of Book Synopsis: a 1-2 page (double-spaced) summary of the book as would be found on the rear side of a published text. This summary should serve to entice readers, encouraging them to buy/read the text, but should not spoil key plot points (such as the ending).

Compare/Contrast: a 2-3 page (double-spaced, MLA formatted) compare & contrast essay discussing the print narrative against its film counterpart. (For texts other than "Minority Report," this requires an outside film viewing of the adaptations of the works).

F. Research Component I. (Traditional Essay): Students will demonstrate synthesis writing and documentation skills through a traditional essay formatted according to MLA standards.

CHOOSE *ONE* OPTION FROM BELOW:

Author Biography: a 2-3 page essay about the author (using proper MLA citation & at least 3 scholarly sources)

Book's Reception: a 2-3 page essay discussing the book's reception/popularity/reviews (using proper MLA citation & at least 3 sources – source types will vary)

Literary Analysis: a 2-3 page essay integrating scholarly research (journal articles), analyzing a key aspect of the text (MLA citation required)

G. Research Component II. (Applied Research Item): Students will demonstrate the ability to research a controversial issue (one highlighted in the text) in order to provide a social commentary (similar or opposite as to that found in the text). Regardless of the option selected below, include a works cited page for this section that lists all of the sources you consulted when crafting this piece.

CHOOSE *ONE* OPTION FROM BELOW:

Public Service Announcement (as would be used by one side of issue in narrative): a public service announcement (print advertisement, faux billboard, commercial, video) advocating for one side of the controversial issue researched (must use material from research).

Poster/Flier/Brochure Advocating One Side of Issue: a print item meant for display/distribution that one side of the issue (supporter or opposition) would utilize to publicize his/her stance on the issue (must include material from research).

PowerPoint Presentation about Debate: a traditional PowerPoint presentation one might use if instructing a class on this controversial issue (must use material from research).

Fig. 1.3. Component Options for Multi-Genre Research Project

Students were assessed by scores earned in each of the seven categories listed above as well as two additional categories based on assembly and design (organization/design and mechanics/writing).

Group Research Presentation

While most of the assessments throughout the course were based on individual accomplishments, one assignment students completed was based on group effort. This collaborative group project allowed students to study a contemporary controversy occurring in the fields of science, law, and/or ethics – one that has infiltrated mainstream media and popular culture. This cooperative learning activity required out of class meetings, research compilation, and a formal group presentation.

Students were able to select from ten different options, and they were placed into two or three person groups based on their interests. These presentations were staggered throughout the semester running from week two until week fourteen. The student presentations were strategically situated within the study of various print or media texts that explored the real-world issue they had studied. The options for research are listed in the table below.

Group 1: The Effects of Social Networking (on Human Relationships / Communication)
Group 2: Artificial Intelligence (The Progress & Potential Outcomes)
Group 3: Plastic Surgery (The Effects of Media Beauty Standards)
Group 4: Global Warming (Human Progress & Environmental Consequences)
Group 5: The Death Penalty (The Debates Concerning Legislation)
Group 6: The Patriot Act (Restricted Freedom, Surveillance, and National Security Issues)

Group 7: Assisted Suicide / Euthanasia (Ethical Debates & Mainstream Examples)
Group 8: Stem Cell Research (Scientific and Political Debates)
Group 9: Cloning (Scientific Accomplishments & Ethical Debates)
Group 10: Human Sex Trafficking (Global Instances & Ethical Debates)

Fig. 1.4. Topics for Group Research Project

After groups were assembled, students researched their assigned topic and crafted a 15-20 minute presentation on the debates surrounding it. Students were required to use five scholarly sources, craft a visual to aid in their presentation, and design a handout with useful information to distribute to their peers. As some of these are controversial issues, students were cautioned to be objective when presenting the material. The purpose of this presentation was not that of a persuasive speech where they would take a stance on the issue but an informative one where they would objectively (and evenly) relay the main points of both sides of the debate without reflecting bias toward one side or the other. Students were assessed on six areas: content (the interest-level and coverage of their assigned topic), research (the variety, balance, and academic quality of their sources), time (mastery of presentation time restrictions), visuals (design and utility of the presentation materials and handouts), organization (the overall structure of the talk and the extent to which the presentation seemed practiced), and delivery (the equal participation of group members and presentation skills among them).

Exams

Beyond the various assignments completed in and out of class, students were also assessed formally by a midterm and final exam. The midterm consisted of two parts: a quote identification section and a short answer section. For the former, students were given ten important quotations from the print and film texts we had studied to date and they were asked to list the title of the text, the name of the author/director, the name of the speaker/narrator, and the overall significance of the quote in relation to the work as a whole. For the latter section, students were given five prompts that asked them to respond to a work's (or a set of works') themes and/or social critique.

While the midterm aimed to assess students' understandings of individual narratives (and their connections to one another), the final exam was focused more on the students' understanding of the course concepts as a whole. This exam took the form of an in-class essay and asked students to respond to the prompt listed below:

Prompt: This course studied narratives that wrestle with ethical concerns surrounding "progress" (societal achievements, technological advancement, scientific discoveries, etc.). The authors and directors of the science fiction/dystopian texts we studied all wove the following questions into their works: what do we do when human survival and societal progress come at extreme costs, and how might such advancements cause us to question our faith in humanity? These authors and directors crafted fictional worlds that serve as cautionary tales for the reader/viewer. They each provided social commentary on various real world, contemporary issues by recreating them, exaggerating them, and situating them within fictional (and oftentimes, futuristic) worlds.

Select texts (based on the requirements below) that you feel well highlight our course theme. In your essay answer the following questions:

- What social commentary are the authors/directors making within each text?
- How well do they carry out these critiques?
- How might their mediated format, genre, and/or time of production influence your evaluation of the texts?
AND
- Are fictional texts a productive site for interrogating these concerns? (If so, why? And, if not, why not, especially when so many fictional texts strive to fulfill this goal?)

Fig. 1.5. Final Exam Essay Prompt

A student earned an "A" on this essay by creating an intriguing, thought provoking response which analyzed all of the required texts in meaningful ways; utilized specific examples to support the argument concerning the overarching theme; thoroughly covered all parts of the essay prompt, and flowed seamlessly, showcasing mastery of organizational devices, language, and proofreading.

Conclusions: The Successes and Challenges in Teaching an Interdisciplinary Course

Overall, the course succeeded in teaching social responsibility as students did begin to show concern about the well-being of various subgroups and the planet as a whole. As research predicted, the fictional narratives were a productive space to engage with controversial topics, and by the end of the term students were able to easily locate the social commentary present within narratives and apply those critiques to the world around them. However, the promise within many scholars' claims that such study would predispose students "to political action" and increase their "political interest and civic tolerance" was not always seen (Hintz and Ostry 8; Evans, Avery, and Pederson 297). While the course may ultimately impact students' political consciousness, there was no way to determine with any accuracy if this will in fact occur. Class discussion and individual writing pieces indicate that students were able to objectively critique the society of which they are a part, but these critiques did not often extend into discussions of how to resolve such cultural problems. For example, while students were quick to agree with scholars who claim that their generation is overly dependent on technology – and students even shared their worries that such dependency could decrease their intellectual capabilities – they never suggested abandoning their favorite technological gadgets, social networking sites, and so forth. However, the fact that these students were able to "evaluate social institutions" and honestly discuss "problems and injustices" is a solid starting place for continued growth (Glasglow 54; Wolk 667).

The only surprising outcome of the course was the lack of group debate it inspired. As a course grounded in supposedly controversial issues, there was an overwhelming consensus on most of the topics. The students almost always agreed with the social commentaries provided by the authors and directors of the various texts and offered very little in terms of counter arguments. Since I have only taught this course one time, I am unable to determine if this was the result of the classroom dynamic, the individual personalities within the class, or if the issues or texts themselves did not cater to divergent viewpoints.

And finally, in terms of the course's cross-curricular focus: I was pleased that students were able to apply the motifs present within the fictional narratives to work being completed in other disciplines. Along the same lines, students were also able to study how these controversial topics were being discussed in other discourses and understand how that conversation – and the research being carried out in diverse fields – was being co-opted by the creators of fictional texts in productive ways.

Works Cited

A.I. Artificial Intelligence. Dir. Steven Spielberg. Writ. Ian Watson. Perf. Haley Joel Osment and Jude Law. Warner Brothers, 2001. DVD.

Aldiss, Brian W. "Super-Toys Last All Summer Long." *Man in His Time: The Best Science Fiction Stories of Brian W. Aldiss.* Ed. Brian W. Aldiss. NY: Atheneum, 1989. 194-201. Print.

Anderson, MT. *Feed.* Cambridge, MA: Candlewick Press, 2002. Print.

Asimov, Isaac. *I, Robot.* NY: Ballantine Books, 1977. Print.

Atwood, Margaret. *The Handmaid's Tale.* NY: Anchor, 1998. Print.

Bauerlein, Mark. *The Dumbest Generation: How the Digital Age Stupefies Young Americans and Jeopardizes Our Future, Or, Don't Trust Anyone Under 30.* NY: Penguin, 2009. Print.

Berman, Sheldon. *Children's Social Consciousness and the Development of Social Responsibility.* Albany, NY: State University of New York Press, 1997. Print.

Blasingame, James. "An Interview with M.T. (Tobin) Anderson." *Journal of Adolescent and Adult Literacy* 47 (September 2003): 98-99. Print.

Carr, Nicholas. "Is Google Making Us Stupid?: What the Internet is Doing to Our Brains." *The Atlantic* July/August 2008. Web. 18 August 2012.

Doctorow, Cory. *Little Brother.* NY: Tor Teen, 2010. Print.

Evans, Ronald W., Patricia G. Avery, and Patricia Velde Pederson. "Taboo Topics: Cultural Restraint on Teaching Social Issues." *The Clearing House* 73.5 (2000): 295-302. Print.

Glasglow, Jaqueline N. "Teaching Social Justice through Young Adult Literature." *The English Journal* 90.6 (2001): 54-61. Print.

Hintz, Carrie, and Elaine Ostry. "Introduction." *Utopian and Dystopian Writing for Children and Young Adults.* Eds. Carrie Hintz and Elaine Ostry. NY: Routledge, 2003. 1-20. Print.

Huxley, Aldous. *Brave New World.* NY: Harper, 2010. Print.

I, Robot. Dir. Alex Proyas. Writ. Jeff Vintar and Akiva Goldsman. Perf. Will Smith and Bridget Moynahan. Twentieth Century Fox, 2004. DVD.

Ishiguro, Kazuo. *Never Let Me Go.* NY: Vintage, 2010. Print

The Island. Dir. Michael Bay. Writ. Caspian Tredwell-Owen and Alex Kurtzman. Perf. Scarlett Johansoon and Ewan McGregor. Dream Works, 2005. DVD.

The Life of David Gale. Dir. Alan Parker. Writ. Charles Randolph. Perf. Kevin Spacey and Kate Winslet. Universal Pictures, 2003. DVD.

Minority Report. Dir. Steven Spielberg. Writ. Scott Frank. Perf. Tom Cruise and Colin Farrell. Twentieth Century Fox, 2002. DVD.

Pace, David. "Controlled Fission: Teaching Supercharged Subjects." *College Teaching* 51.2 (2003): 42-45. Print.

Payne, Brian K., and Randy R. Gainey. "Understanding and Developing Controversial Issues in College Courses." *College Teaching* 51.2 (2003): 52-58. Print.

Repo Men. Dir. Miguel Sapochnik. Writ. Eric Garcia and Garrett Lerner. Perf. Jude Law and Forest Whitaker. Universal Pictures, 2010. DVD.

Scott, Kristi N., and M. Heather Dragoo. "The Baroque Body: A Social Commentary on the Role of Body Modification in Scott Westerfeld's Uglies Trilogy." *Academia.edu.* 2011. Web. 25 July 2011.

Westerfeld, Scott. *Uglies.* NY: Simon Pulse, 2011. Print.

Wolk, Steven. "Reading for a Better World: Teaching for Social Responsibility with Young Adult Literature." *Journal of Adolescent & Adult Literacy* 52.8 (2009): 664-673. Print.

SECTION II:

THE BODY IN POPULAR DISCOURSE

CHAPTER SEVEN

SELLING WEDDINGS AND PRODUCING BRIDES: MEDIATED PORTRAYALS OF THAT "PERFECT DAY"

SARAH HIMSEL BURCON

"Many women want to have weddings: few of them want to be wives."
Dale Spender (ed.), *Weddings and Wives (cover)*

Introduction

During the past 20 years, the American public has witnessed an increased interest in self-improvement, and finding the "perfect mate" is certainly on the agenda of many women: marriage, many believe, offers women a sense of self-fulfillment, a feeling of being more complete. The entertainment industry has helped to both initiate and foster this interest by offering consumers various products – magazines, television shows, films, literature, and so forth – thus assisting the public with these self-improvements. This chapter examines some of these mediated products surrounding weddings by, first, offering a brief historical overview of American nuptials. The chapter argues that America in general is becoming entrenched in a didactic, how-to culture, and more specifically, American women in particular are heeding this instructive material given their focus on creating their fairy tale perfect day – a focus that is largely constructed by a society that advises them of its necessity. Furthermore, the chapter demonstrates how these cultural products often work to reinforce the traditional status quo that situates women in the domestic realm, rather than to resist stereotypes by offering up stronger models of femininity during the wedding phase.[1]

---

[1] It should be noted that this chapter focuses on heterosexual marriages simply because of their lengthy history. However, doing so does not indicate a privileging

According to Chrys Ingraham in her text, *White Weddings: Romancing Heterosexuality in Popular Culture*, weddings are an important, albeit largely unexplored, site of study. Ingraham maintains:

> weddings are culturally pervasive, symbolically prolific, and are rarely questioned or examined. Yet, they are so taken for granted they seem naturally occurring and function to naturalize a host of heterosexual behaviors that are, in fact, socially produced. In other words, *one is not born a bride or with the desire to become a bride* yet we have an abundance of evidence that shows that many people believe otherwise. (3-4, emphasis in original)

Ingraham's overall thesis in her text, as her title highlights, is that weddings work to privilege heterosexuality. Additionally, and significant to this chapter, is Ingraham's argument about the misperception in American culture that, from childhood, women possess an intrinsic desire to be married. Indeed, just as this was not the case historically, it is also not true today.

Ellen Rothman, in a historical study of American courtship titled *Hands and Hearts*, supports the claim that women are *not* born "with the desire to become a bride."[2] Going back several years, Rothman asserts that women in colonial America considered marriage as simply a part of life rather than a major change. At this time in history, "the demands of an agricultural existence provided continuity" in that a young woman "would do the milking in her husband's barn rather than her father's, but the tasks and setting were unchanged" (74). However, this changed at the end of the 18th century given the shift from subsistence farming to a more urban existence. At this time, "the traditional division of labor was fast becoming a separation of 'spheres'": rather than helping her husband on the farm, a woman now worked inside the home. (Rothman 74). The late 18th century – after the Revolution – also brought with it "the ideal of Republican Motherhood" which emerged "to preserve patriarchal authority while assigning to women the all-important task of rearing patriotic citizens...Her husband and children would look to her for the purity, piety, submissiveness, and domesticity that were expected of a True Woman" (Rothman 66). Thus, it is at this time that women became more cut off from their families and more dependent on their husbands for security,

---

of heterosexual marriage over homosexual marriage, thus reinforcing heteronormativity.
[2] Rothman offers a useful distinction between *courting* and *courtship*: courtship is used in reference to situations in which couples intend to marry, while courting does not always result in marriage (23).

while at the same time they were responsible for the domestic realm (Rothman 67). Thus, although the men of late 18th century may have considered marriage as "their chance to *have* a home," young women, on the other hand, "saw it as a separation *from* home" (Rothman 69, emphasis in original). Because of this separation anxiety, many women attempted to delay the engagement for lengthy periods of time.[3]

If it is true that women were not exactly clamoring to get married 200 years ago, the question becomes: when, and why, did women begin thinking obsessively about their wedding day? Or, when did society determine that finding a husband and having an elaborate wedding were uppermost on every woman's mind beginning in childhood? To answer these questions, it is important to offer a brief historical look at weddings.

Weddings, American Style

Eighteenth century weddings in America were relatively private affairs. Ceremonies were generally held at the home of the bride or groom's parents, as opposed to in churches given the Puritans' belief that marriage was a civil ceremony rather than a religious rite. Similarly, early nineteenth century weddings were usually simple affairs, with the couple spending little time in the planning and preparation; often, invitations were sent out only about a week before the wedding (Rothman 77-78). At the end of the 18th century, many weddings still took place at the bride's home, although some couples were now opting for church weddings. By the middle of the 19th century, weddings became more elaborate affairs; printed wedding invitations, for example, were sent out weeks in advance, and instead of inviting only a few people, the couple might invite 200 people to share in their nuptials (Rothman 168-169). But by the end of the nineteenth century, large church weddings became standard for couples (Rothman 78), and this trend has continued into the present. Accompanying this shift toward the larger wedding celebration has been, expectedly, an increase in wedding-related spending. In terms of cost: during the past two centuries at least, American weddings have transitioned from a simple affair to a much more extravagant spectacle. The escalation of wedding expenses can be seen most obviously toward the end of the 20th century. For example, in 1945 couples spent on average $2,240 on their wedding ("The Wedding Report"), and in 1984,

---

[3] Rothman notes that diaries of women from the 1780s to the 1830s reveal the trepidation they felt upon their impending marriages: they were, for example, "anxious," "mortified," and "fretful" (72).

they spent about $4,000 (Otnes and Pleck 2). Surprisingly, this is not much of an increase considering the 40-year time span in between. But in 1994, the average cost soared to $14,000, which is almost four times the amount from ten years earlier (Otnes and Pleck 2). Today, the average cost has reached a plateau: in 2007 the average spent on a wedding was $28,730 ("The Wedding Report"), and, similarly, in 2012 it was $28,427 (Hicken).

Several reasons might account for this increased spending toward the end of the 20th century and into the 21st. One possible reason is that, often, both members of the couple were employed in 1994, as opposed to in 1984. As such, they could pay more for their wedding. Another reason is the increased use of credit cards, which made it easier to spend more now and pay later. Still another reason can be attributed to the entertainment industry's portrayals of weddings and brides that cause people – women in particular, considering they are the target audience – to want to spend more in order to have their fairytale wedding. Elizabeth Pleck and Cele Otnes in *Cinderella Dreams: The Allure of the Lavish Wedding* suggest that it was in the 1920s that the phrase "the perfect wedding" became popular. They claim that "Standards of perfection…were created by advertisers, marketers, and bridal magazines. Couples were urged to buy expensive engraved invitations, proper-vintage champagne, an ornate wedding cake, and of course, the perfect designer gown" (Otnes and Pleck 18). They offer as support various advertisements from a 1920s issue of *Modern Bride*: for example, an ad from Pier One Imports: "Register for the gifts that make your home *perfect* together"; from Gingiss Formalwear: "Make Your Day *Picture Perfect*; and from J.C. Penney Bridal Registry's: "The *Perfect* Match" (Otnes and Pleck 18-19, emphasis added).

Bridal Magazines: Advertisements as Reinforcement of the Status Quo

Magazines in general are an important area of study given their large and varied audiences, and, certainly, bridal magazines are also significant given their target audience of exclusively women. The first magazine devoted specifically to brides was *Bride's Magazine*, published for the first time in Autumn of 1934.[4] In *Decoding Women's Magazines*, Ellen McCracken notes that corporations like Conde Nast, publisher of *Bride's Magazine*, determined that weddings, which are important events in one's

---

[4] The title of the magazine when it was originally published was *Bride's*; later, it was titled *Brides*.

lifetime, are "especially lucrative times to bring advertisers' messages to female consumers"; furthermore, magazines can serve to "instill a large array of pseudo-needs in women" during the time surrounding this important event in their lives.   Problematically, many of these messages and indoctrinated needs were heavily entrenched in popularly-held heteronormative, patriarchal societal norms common at the time of publication (268). McCracken discusses the October/November issue from a 1983 *Bride's* that she claims "[presented] stereotypical models for women, and attempted to anchor certain dominant social mores. The feature 'Becoming a Wife', for example, [advised] readers how to assume the new role that [would] be expected of them" (MacCracken 269). As such, she concludes, *Bride's Magazine*, along with *Modern Bride*, "[upheld] the traditional status quo ideologically at the same time that they [taught] readers to purchase numerous commodities" – commodities that would ensure that they would fall in line with such ideological norms (McCracken 269-270).

    Although one would hope that more contemporary issues of *Brides Magazine* do not continue this practice of associating soon-to-be married women with conventional domestic roles, unfortunately, this practice continues.   For example, the October/November 2013 issue includes various ads that do just this. One ad for Cuisinart depicts a future groom, on bent knee, proposing to his would-be bride. He has painted "Will you marry me?" on the wall, and his fiancé reacts as one might expect: she is thrilled. The copy reads:

> One good proposal deserves another! Not that he's popped the question, it's time to say 'yes' to the kitchen of your dreams. So, when filling out your registry, pick something fast, that's build to last, something hot, like a set of pots, and something new that's brewed just for you. Make the kitchen of your dreams a reality with Cuisinart. (Cuisinart 160-161)

This ad highlights at least three issues: first, the sentence "Now that he's popped the question, it's time to say 'yes' to the kitchen of your dreams" places the romantic ideal of the wedding on the same level as domesticity, implying that, for the woman, the wedding and the domestic realm exist (or should exist) in tandem. Also, the word "dream" appears twice in the ad, further inculcating in women the notion of living in a fairytale world once married. Finally, the singsong, rhyming nature of the ad, along with the reference to the "something borrowed, something blue," serve to both infantilize women and perpetuate the prospective fairytale-like quality of the wedding that women are meant to embrace.

A Macy's ad in the same issue features a young man and his bride-to-be sitting on a couch, surrounded by gift registry items such as home appliances and towels. This ad, too, glamorizes domesticity: the future bride is wearing a tiara, implying she is a princess who has snagged her prince. At the same time, she is surrounded by blenders, cake plates, dishes, pots, and towels, and the copy urges the couple to "Register for Macy's Dream Fund" (Macy's 54). In this ad, both the images and the text suggest a merging of the romantic with the domestic. On the second page of this two-page ad is a full-sized image of two Dyson vacuums (meant to represent the couple), along with flowers in a vase in between the two vacuums. The words "I do" are in the upper right hand corner, and the copy reads: "Make a clean sweep as you start your new life together" (Macy's 55). The "I do," placed strategically over the bright pink vacuum cleaner, along with the pink flowers, work together to imply that she will say "I do" to her fiancé at the same time that she says "I do" to the domestic realm. Essentially, the message here is that a bride-to-be can be a princess, provided that she combines this glamorous role with the soon-to-be domestic role of wife. This is ironic, of course, considering that fairytale mythology would have us believe that the prince is supposed to take the young woman away from a life of toil so that she can become a princess. Finally, the juxtaposition of "dream fund" with "the magic of Macy's" works as a method to remind the bride-to-be that her wedding should combine the magic – found through marriage –with her childhood dreams of becoming a bride (Macy's 54-55). Hence, similar to the Cuisinart ad, the Macy's ad also infantilizes women and upholds domestic stereotypes.

Yet another contemporary advertisement worthy of study is one for cookware found in the Winter 2014 issue of *Martha Stewart Weddings*. The ad for All-Clad shows a young bride-to-be holding a large frying pan in front of her body, and the copy below her chin reads: "I fell for a rugged, real looker who cleans up good. Now we're together for life" (137). The copy indicates that, along with falling for her future husband, the future bride has also fallen for the cookware. That is, the perfect marriage for a woman is one that *unites* her with a man at the same time that it *unites* her to her new world of household tasks. While the copy on the first page of this two page ad stresses the rewards of cooking together with a spouse, the fact that the woman is holding the cookware and the copy states they are "together for life" suggests that the domestic realm is exclusively her domain. Although the ad is intended to be humorous, it still works as any ad from 50 years ago might work in that it reinforces stereotypical models for women.

What is significant about all three of the ads discussed here is that they use direct address to communicate (supposedly veiled) directives: Cuisinart tells the future bride to "Make the kitchen of *your* dreams a reality with Cuisinart" (Cuisinart 161, emphasis added); the Macy's ad tells her to "make a clean sweep as *you* start *your* new life together" (Macy's 55, emphasis added); and the All-Clad ad maintains that "Expressing *your* culinary side is fulfilling while creating a recipe and also when enjoying the results at the table" (All-Clad 136, emphasis added). Interestingly enough, using direct address is something the self-help genre does as well. Although most people would not consider bridal magazines as a part of the self-help genre, the childlike rhetoric, the rhyming tone, and the use of direct address suggest otherwise.

Social Media: Producing the Perfect Spectacle

But before they purchase the many advertised household items, women must first buy the wedding dress. In 2012, women in America spent on average $1200 on their dresses (Hall and Jury). However, this is not much compared to what celebrities spend on their dresses, celebrities many women would like to emulate. Celebrity weddings and royal weddings have certainly promoted the desire in ordinary women to want the perfect wedding and the perfect dress. For example, people were fascinated by Queen Victoria and Prince Albert's wedding in 1840, and it is because of her example that today women typically wear a white wedding gown. In *Marriage, a History*, Stephanie Coontz remarks on this fact:

> [Queen Victoria] broke with convention and walked down the aisle to musical accompaniment, wearing pure white instead of the traditional silver and white gown and colored cape, [creating] an overnight 'tradition'. Thousands of middle-class women imitated her example, turning their weddings into the most glamorous event of their lives, an elaborate celebration of their entry into respectable domesticity. (167)

Of course, white is also associated with purity, which was significant especially prior to the mid-20th century (before what is now known as second wave feminism), when brides were supposed to remain pure up until their wedding night.[5] Rothman maintains that the elaborate wedding

---

[5] Veils became popular in the 1840s and, not surprisingly, women began wearing them "at the same time that women were being elevated to a pedestal by a culture that defined womanhood in terms of 'purity, piety, submissiveness, and domesticity'" (Rothman 171)

acted as a reward of sorts for women who remained virgins up until their wedding and also helped to mitigate the sting of abandoning their ambitions in favor of their husbands' (Otnes and Pleck 7). Although this may have been true during Victorian times, Otnes and Pleck claim that

> applying it to contemporary culture suggests that as bridal virginity has disappeared, and as women's employment opportunities have approximated those available to men, the lavish wedding should have become superfluous....Obviously, these assumptions have not been supported in recent history, as nonvirgins with independent incomes, now the bridal majority, not only contribute to the weddings of their dreams but also have redefined the meaning of white as a symbol of tradition rather than of purity. *In short, the demand for lavish weddings has increased even in the face of women's increased education, income-earning ability, and political participation.* (7, emphasis added)

All one has to do is look at average wedding costs to see that, indeed, weddings are still lavish, even though women are more educated, are earning more, and are (likely) more politically savvy than in the past. This all suggests that a wedding, lavish or otherwise, is no longer a reward. Rather, it is more of a necessity to many people, and women in particular, given its "once-in-a-lifetime" status promoted by cultural products such as bridal magazines.

It is interesting to speculate on why having an elaborate wedding is appealing in this transition to marriage. Otnes and Pleck argue that the lavish wedding during most of the 20th century

> appeals to dreams, wishes, and fantasies stirred by romantic consumer culture. It appeals because couples and their families are trying to take goods, services, and experiences and turn them into symbols of romantic love...Through artifacts, photography, and videography, the lavish wedding is supposed to generate lasting memories that become not only the way the event is remembered, but also a way of keeping alive the belief in romantic love even when the flames of passion begin to flicker. With the growth of video and computer technology, ordinary couples not only can emulate celebrity lifestyles on their own wedding day but also can point to the videos and photographs that captured their star status for years to come. (Otnes and Pleck 267)

Some noteworthy ideas here are, first, the extravagant wedding that many women dream of, beginning in childhood or not, can be linked to romance: the "perfect" wedding matches the "perfect" romance felt by the couple. Also significant is the notion that women wish to obtain "star status," even if only for one day. As was mentioned previously, Queen Victoria's wedding changed the course of weddings, but since that time, many other weddings have done the same. In 1956, Prince Rainier married Grace Kelly, who wore a dress made from "25 yards of silk taffeta, 100 yards of silk net, 125-year-old rose-point lace bought from a museum and thousands of tiny pearls" (Haydon). Other notable weddings were those of Marilyn Monroe and Joe DiMaggio in 1954; John F. Kennedy and Jacqueline Lee Bouvier in 1953; and then, of course, the wedding that anyone born after 1970 would likely remember: the nuptials of Lady Diana Spencer and Prince Charles on July 29, 1981, which was televised to over 750 million viewers (Haydon).[6] The most recent wedding that drew an audience estimated at 2.4 billion people (global television and online) was that of Prince William and Kate Middleton in April of 2012. Middleton's dress, for this most publically consumed wedding to date, in itself alludes back to the long tradition of the mass following of celebrity weddings. Her lace and ivory gown was designed by Sarah Burton, and many remarked on its similarity to Grace Kelly's dress ("Royal Wedding 2011"). These weddings drew wide audiences in large part because of their spectacle-like quality, but also, as was maintained here, because women wanted to emulate celebrity or royal weddings.

Today, more than ever before, it is easier to do this. With the rise of social media (e.g., Facebook Twitter, blogs, YouTube, Snapchat, and so forth), everyday people are able to have their 15 minutes of fame that Andy Warhol spoke of almost 50 years ago. They can now document any part of their lives, no matter how insignificant it is, and weddings, which are significant, can therefore receive even more attention than before. This turn toward social media serves at least two purposes: it leads to a more narcissistic culture in that, 10 years ago, a wedding was an important event in a couple's life, but now, everything related to it – the proposal, the planning, and so forth – is much more of a spectacle. Social media allows the couple to immediately notify their friends and family of the smallest details. But at the same time, because there are so many types of social media and so much emphasis is placed on using social media for any event, couples might feel compelled to utilize these outlets when planning a wedding; as such, the existence of social media might be said to act in a fashion similar to the advertisements in the sense that they are instructing

---

[6] Another famous wedding from 1981 was that of a fictitious television couple. However, it might as well have been an actual ceremony given its audience of more than 30 million people. This was the wedding between two characters from the ABC soap opera, *General Hospital*: Luke Spencer (Anthony Geary) and Laura Webber Baldwin (Genie Francis). This episode was the "highest-rated hour in soap-opera history" (Haydon).

couples in how to create their fairytale wedding, along with the events
leading up to it.[7]

The Brides of Reality TV

Of course, most women do not have weddings on the same scale as
celebrities. But for some women, being on a television reality show is the
next best thing. Enter shows such as *The Bachelorette* (which documents a
woman's path toward a marriage proposal), *Say Yes to the Dress* (which
focuses specifically on women's quest to find the ultimate wedding
accessory), and the two examined here: *Bridezillas* and *A Wedding Story*.
In these shows, all of which offer a consumer-driven focus, everyday
women are turned into *faux* celebrities for their viewing audience. Each
episode of *Bridezillas* (WEtv, 2004 - 2013), tells the stories of two brides-
to-be. The brides' stories begin with the bride and groom telling how they
met and fell in love. But the stories, in general, focus on the arguments and
negative interactions between the "bridezilla" – who is depicted as a self-
centered, emotional bully – and her groom-to-be, her family, and her
friends.

In the episode titled "Jeanine and Rochelle" (Season 9, episode 4),
viewers meet 18 year old Rochelle and her fiancé, Nathan, along with
Jeanine and her fiancé, Thomas. Both women are shown to be
temperamental, selfish, and egotistical, and both have timid fiancés who
allow themselves to be ordered around. Rochelle, or "baby zilla" as she is
sometimes amusingly referred to by the show's narrator, proudly relays at
the beginning of the show, when asked about her job, that she "doesn't do
anything" ("Jeanine and Rochelle"). Nathan, who is in the Army, is
stationed in Alaska, which makes theirs a long distance relationship.
Rochelle shows her selfish side when talking about the wedding budget
with her mother, defiantly telling her: "I want what I want" ("Jeanine and
Rochelle"). Similarly, Jeanine tells her audience that she "[likes] to be in
control...at all times" because "there's a lot of areas (*sic*) that [Thomas]
drops the ball on" ("Jeanine and Rochelle"). Although he appears ready to
marry this zilla, Thomas knows his friends and family don't like Jeanine.
In fact, he says his family is "anti-Jeanine 100%" ("Jeanine and
Rochelle").

While the audience does not see the actual wedding of Rochelle and
Nathan, they do see Jeanine and Thomas's. After the "I do's," Jeanine

---

[7] See, for example, the 30 minute proposal on YouTube titled "Justin and Emily:
The Proposal," which is likened to a reality show and which has gone viral.

continues behaving badly at the reception. Having learned that her father-in-law, Joe, has taken her own father home at his request, Jeanine throws a tantrum and tells Joe he has to leave as well. It is only at this point that Thomas sees his bride's true character and throws his ring at her. In the end he finally confronts her, telling her that she needs to "shut up," that she's being "disrespectful" ("Jeanine and Rochelle"). The show ends with Joe commenting that the wedding "went better than expected" due to, of course, the break up ("Jeanine and Rochelle").

Quite obviously this television show, and many others like it, speaks to our consumer culture in that the spectacle of the event and the lavishness are celebrated. The question one might consider after watching a program replete with narcissistic brides and spineless grooms – certainly not a "feel good" kind of show in the traditional sense– is: why does it have such a huge fan base? One theory behind the popularity of reality television programming featuring people behaving badly falls in line with the concept of *schadenfreude*, the notion that people often rejoice in the humiliation and misery of others (Pozner 16). In the case of these specific shows, the audience might be looking at the characters and the situations and thinking smugly to themselves that they are "nothing like that." Women in particular might admit that they get a little crazy over wedding planning, but *Bridezillas* takes this insanity to the next level: as executive producer Laura Halperin commented, "sometimes the ladies take things just a little too seriously" (Italie). Indeed, this is an understatement. But what is noteworthy about this program is that, while female viewers might maintain that they are nothing like these bridezillas they are laughing at, at the same time, such exaggerated portrayals of reality TV brides might work to do two things: such portrayals might allow female viewers to distance themselves from such behavior, *or* these portrayals might make the bad behavior of real women seem normal by comparison. In both of these instances, *Bridezillas* acts as a didactic narrative in that it either tells the bride how *not* to act, or it tells the bride that her behavior is much better compared to the brides of reality television.

Another reality show about weddings is *A Wedding Story* (TLC, 1996 - present). In this program the audience is made to feel as if they are simply viewing a home video of a couple. However, in reality, this program is "carefully constructed around a precise format that culminated in a clichéd fairy-tale ending" (Stephens 195). *A Wedding Story* shows the couple talking about their lives together up until this point and, according to Rebecca Stephens, author of *Understanding Reality Television*:

> there are significant correlations between the show and traditional female fantasies under socially normalized gender roles. The most obvious is in

the fairy-tale ending of each episode, a visual equivalent of 'happily ever after' that is frequently marked as well by images of feminine submission. (196)

Stephens offers an analysis of one episode in particular, titled "Becky and Joe" (2002), that is exemplary of this. In this episode, the bride and groom marry in a "medieval/Renaissance-themed wedding," and the show ends with

> a mock kidnapping where the groom must fight the 'bad guys' (his groomsmen) to 'reclaim' his bride; the credits close with Joe carrying Becky out of the reception slung over his shoulder. There is also a continued implicit emphasis on a male-provider model of marriage, gifts of jewellery appear again and again and close-up shots of rings are *de rigueur*. (Stephens 196).

As was stated previously with regard to the advertisements that are perhaps meant to be amusing: what is problematic here is that these cultural products still manage to perpetuate gender stereotypes, despite the intent to be amusing.

In *Reality Bites: The Troubling Truth about Guilty Pleasure TV*, Jennifer Pozner discusses the detrimental effects of such programming, particularly on female viewers. She also notes the draw of *schadenfreude* and the escapist appeal (as seen in the recurrent fairytale motifs), but argues that while those may get viewers to tune in initially, that is not what holds their attention (Pozner 17). Pozner suggests:

> on a more subconscious level, we continue to watch because these shows frame their narratives in ways that both play to and reinforce deeply ingrained societal biases about women and men, love and beauty, race and class, consumption and happiness in America. (17)

One major societal message that surfaces in reality television is associated with the antifeminist backlash ideology. The tactic by which this message is hammered home most regularly is humiliation. Be it the "star" of the dating shows like *The Bachelor/Bachelorette* or the wedding-spectacle shows like *Bridezillas*, the strategic humiliation of female reality television characters is often "used to offer women an ugly, unstated, and all-too-clear message: "This is where independence leads, ladies – to failure and misery" (Pozner 53).

In the reality television dating shows (such as *The Bachelor/ Bachelorette*) this is particularly obvious. The practice can be seen when the "cameras zoom in on the tear-soaked face of some woman shattered by romantic rejection. Producers bank on such scenes to reinforce the notion that single women are whimpering spinsters who can never be fulfilled without husbands" (Pozner 55). The strategic editing of such shows, such as the infamous "Frankenbiting" (wherein the actual words of onscreen persons are edited so that they come across as saying almost the opposite of what they really said), also paints women in a negative light. Pozner notes that women get

> edited into stock reality TV characters: The Weeper, whose self-doubt is played for laughs. The Antagonizer, whose confidence is framed as arrogance. The Slut, whose strategic use of sex appeal we're meant to condemn. Through their beauty-based bravado and anxiety, participants become vessels on whose bodies and from whose lips these shows can reinforce antifeminist backlash values. (72)

So while reality television shows are not often cast explicitly into the self-help realm like traditional dating guides, or consumed for similar reasons as is the case for bridal magazines, these programs are acting in the same vein. While they are not always explicitly telling women how to act in order to become a bride, or as a bride, they are implicitly instructing them in this way: they are cautioning them on behaviors to avoid, privileging various practices, and reinforcing normative ideologies.

Brides of the Big Screen

While celebrity weddings or weddings of "real" people (on reality television) are certainly significant indicators of how weddings do look or should look, so too are the fictionalized portrayals of brides and weddings important when considering depictions of brides and grooms. Some of the many recent movies that do this are Clare Kilner's *The Wedding Date* (2005), Sanaa Hamri's *Something New* (2006), Anne Fletcher's *27 Dresses* (2008), Michael Patrick King's *Sex and the City* (2008), Paul Feig's *Bridesmaids* (2011), and Luke Greenfield's *Something Borrowed* (2011) to name a few. Here, the focus is on two films, *Sex and the City* and *27 Dresses,* in large part due to their box office success.

Sex and the City (HBO, 1998-2004) experienced massive success as a television show. The series, along with the director, several actors, and crew members, were nominated for and/or won numerous awards during its run: it won, for example, Golden Globe awards for Best TV Series in 2000, 2001, and 2002 and an Emmy award for Outstanding Comedy Series in 2001. Sarah Jessica Parker won Golden Globe awards for Best Actress in 2000, 2001, 2002, and 2004, and several of the cast and crew members were nominated for awards as well. The television show can arguably be considered a "dating show" that in many ways instructed women on how to behave on the dating market. *Sex and the City* the film picks up where the TV series left off with the lives and loves of four friends: Carrie Bradshaw (Sarah Jessica Parker), Samantha Jones (Kim Cattrall), Charlotte York (Kristin Davis), and Miranda Hobbes (Cynthia Nixon). Unlike the television show, the film morphs into a portrayal of the many issues a bride-to-be faces when planning a wedding. The story begins with Carrie, a NYC columnist at *Vogue*, reflecting back on her life as a "20-something" woman who, like many other 20-something women, went "to NY for two words that begin with 'L': labels and love" (*Sex and the City*). The film is largely about Carrie and "Mr. Big's" (her partner, played by Chris Noth) decision to get married after a 10-year relationship. Although two of Carrie's three friends are excited about the prospect of her being married, one friend, Samantha, points out the potential problems with marriage. In one scene Carrie tells Samantha she has some news for her, and Samantha reacts excitedly with the hope that Carrie is finally considering Botox. When she finds out Carrie's actual news, she unenthusiastically replies: "Well, that's great....Honey, you know me. I don't really believe in marriage. Now Botox, on the other hand, that works every time" (*Sex and the City*). Samantha, of course, could be speaking for many who believe in proven results, which marriage does not always provide.

Although the film does have a happily-ever-after ending, there are some bumps along the way. Miranda learns of her husband's infidelity (although it was "just once"), which causes her to split with him for a short time. However, the big news is that, as the wedding gets more elaborate – going from 75 guests to 200; from an inexpensive, simple gown to a beautiful designer gown; from a somewhat obscure, small event to a much-publicized event – Carrie's fiancé becomes increasingly tense, which sets in motion his eventual act of leaving her at the altar. The publicity is due to Carrie's boss, editor of *Vogue*, Enid Frick (Candice Bergen), telling Carrie that she wants her to be featured in *Vogue* as "The Last Single Girl," complete with photographs of Carrie wearing multiple designer bridal gowns. When Carrie denies that she is the "last single girl," Frick replies, humorously, "No, but 40 is the last age a woman can be photographed in a wedding gown without the unintended Diane Arbus subtext" (*Sex and the City*), echoing, it would seem, years of similar thinking in popular culture as to the "correct" age a woman should marry – and wear white – at her wedding.

At the end of the film, Carrie, after finally forgiving Big for leaving her at the altar due to his fear of marriage changing everything, comments: "we were perfectly happy until we decided to live happily ever after" (*Sex and the City*). This is meant to emphasize how the couple can easily lose track of the reason they are getting married once the wedding becomes an attempt to submit to popular culture's idea of the idealized fairytale wedding. However, the film is worthy of critique because it seems to do the opposite of what it might have set out to do. That is, instead of critiquing the wedding industry along with the hysteria surrounding weddings, it perpetuates common myths and prescriptive behavior: consider, for example, Big getting cold feet, which prompts Carrie to behave in the stereotypical nurturing role, thus ensuring he can settle into the domestic realm that marriage provides.

Another film that highlights weddings is *27 Dresses* (2008). In this romantic comedy, Jane Nichols (Katherine Heigl) has found her "calling" in life at age 8: she helps brides at their weddings and thus becomes the quintessential bridesmaid. At one of these weddings she meets Kevin Doyle (James Marsden), who will at the end of the film become her husband. But, of course, this does not happen until the conventional love triangle is resolved. Jane has been in love with her boss, George (Edward Burns) for quite some time, but when her sister Tess (Malin Akerman) shows up, George falls for her instead, and the two decide to marry. Kevin, the reporter who is to cover their wedding, learns of Jane's fascination with weddings and decides to write, under a pseudonym, about Jane, the "perennial bridesmaid," in order to possibly get promoted.

From the beginning, the viewer witnesses Kevin's cynicism about weddings. He tells his boss, when discussing the article he plans to write about Jane:

> This woman has been in 27 weddings... this year. But it won't just be about her. It will be an incisive look at how the wedding industry has transformed something that should be an important rite of passage into nothing more than a revenue stream. (*27 Dresses*)

Although Kevin thinks weddings can be an "important rite of passage," he does not necessarily consider them romantic. And clearly, he is not partial to the wedding industry.

Jane, on the other hand, does see the romance in weddings. But she also looks at participating in weddings as "being there for a friend" (*27 Dresses*). The following interchange with Kevin demonstrates this:

Jane: I don't care if somebody wants me to wear a funny dress. It's their day, not mine.
Kevin: What about you? You don't have any needs?
Jane: Someday, God knows when, someday, it'll be my day. Then all those people will be there for me. (*27 Dresses*)

Thus, wearing the dresses and being a bridesmaid is, for Jane, about being there for a friend on a day that she has dreamed about since she was a little girl.

The deciding factor for Jane and Kevin is when they realize they have more in common than they had first imagined. Jane asks Kevin if there is anything at all that he likes about weddings, and he responds: "When the bride comes in and she makes her giant grand entrance. I like to glance back at the poor bastard getting married because even though I think he's an idiot for willingly entering into the last legal form of slavery, he always looks really, really happy" (*27 Dresses*). Jane had said something similar to this in a prior scene, and it is this shared idea about weddings that eventually unites them.

Both *Sex and the City* and *27 Dresses* are romantic comedies, and as such audiences understand that the storylines are not to be taken too seriously. That said, there are differences between the two films that are noteworthy in terms of feminist analysis and the subject of whether weddings work to emphasize or subvert longstanding patriarchal stereotypes. Many reviewers of *27 Dresses* remarked on its unremarkable nature as a film, although they had a great deal to say about its overall message: in *Entertainment Weekly*, for example, Owen Gleiberman maintains:

> *27 Dresses* is a movie geared to a pitch of high matrimonial-princess fever. It's white-lace porn for girls of every age, and the way that it revels in that get-me-to-the-altar mood, to the point of making anyone who *isn't* getting married feel like a loser, is the picture's key selling point...Even the satire of the wedding industry plays like a backhanded endorsement of it. (Gleiberman)

And Ann Homaday in the *Washington Post* laments that "There is not one surprising, charming or endearingly quirky thing about "27 Dresses".... This is a movie that actually invokes the term 'Bridezilla' as if it's a brand-new idea instead of a ready-for-retirement cliché." Certainly, both of these reviewers have touched on some key points discussed throughout this chapter. First, movies such as *27 Dresses* maintain the status quo that says women should get married because it is simply the expected thing to do; after all, they have been told that they have dreamed of this day since childhood. Also, similar to the *Bridezillas* reality show previously discussed, *27 Dresses* is ultimately suggesting that it is fine, even expected, for a woman to behave in a neurotic fashion when the end goal is marriage (consider, for example, the montage scene in which Heigl is trying on all of her dresses, one after another). In this way, *27 Dresses* acts as a didactic text instructing women on acceptable and unacceptable behavior when planning their nuptials.

Sex and the City is a bit more interesting, however, in terms of a feminist analysis. Certainly, critics have read this film as upholding gender stereotypes. On the other hand, Alice Wignall in her review titled "Can a Feminist Really Love *Sex and the City*?" offers a useful assessment of the film (along with the television show). Her answer to the question posed in the title is, in short, "yes, she can." Wignall states that the reason the television show was not "embraced by the sisterhood as must-see feminist TV" is because "for a show about women, it displays a singular obsession with men" (Wignall). With reference to the film: Wignall cites scholars such as Janet MCabe (co-editor of *Reading Sex and the City*) as saying that the four women in *Sex and the City* "are still caught in fairytale narratives" (qtd. in Wignall). Furthermore, Imelda Whelehan (author of *From Sex and the Single Girl to Sex and the City*) opines: "It does seem that, in the end, it had to come back to a traditional view…That the future for most women means marriage and children" (qtd in Wignall). To counter this, Wignal points out how both the television show and the film tackle several serious issues, such as infertility, single motherhood, sexual discrimination, and divorce. Additionally:

> The success of SATC showed that, at the very least, there's still plenty of mileage in the tension between independence and the desire for sex, love and partnership; and especially for all those things with men. These questions are not dealt with in an unintelligent way; the chorus of different female voices is a useful device for discussing them; that it fails to offer any novel answers is a function of the fact that it is, after all, just a TV fairy story. It also seems churlish to be bitter about the fact that Carrie *et al* do not offer a fail-safe model for emancipated womanhood when nor, frankly, has real-life feminism.

It seems that the difference between *27 Dresses* and *Sex and the City* is that the former willingly participates in the fairytale version of weddings, thus reinforcing the status quo, while the latter, perhaps while participating in stereotypes, at the very least exposes them for what they are and contributes to conversations about some important subjects relating to women in the 21st century.

Conclusion

Magazines, television shows, and films that focus on weddings are not necessarily a negative thing; indeed, their content is oftentimes humorous and entertaining. However, it is important, as consumers of these mediated products, to analyze and read these materials with a critical eye. Every day young girls and women are being inundated with information that instructs them on various gendered behaviors. For example, when a young woman looks at a magazine showing a beautiful woman in a beautiful wedding dress, standing next to a kitchen appliance, this sends a signal to her that marriage and domesticity go hand in hand. Or when she watches a film in which the bride-to-be gets her perfect mate even though (or perhaps, because) she has behaved irrationally, this, too sends a message. Hence, it is crucial to closely read to these cultural products – to be an active participant in "the chorus of different female voices" (Wignall) – in order to challenge existing societal standards.

Works Cited

27 Dresses. Dir. Anne Fletcher. Perf. Katharine Heigl and James Marsden. 20th Century Fox, 2008. Video.

All-Clad. Advertisement. *Martha Stewart Weddings.* Winter 2014: 136-137. Print.

Coontz, Stephanie. Marriage, a History: How Love Conquered Marriage. New York: Penguin, 2005. Print.

Cuisinart. Advertisement. *Brides Magazine.* Oct./Nov. 2013: 160-161. Print

Gleiberman, Owen. Rev. of *27 Dresses,* dir. Anne Fletcher. *Entertainment Weekly.* 16 January 2008. Web. 22 January 2013.

Hall, Michelle, and Lizzie Jury. "I Do…Cost a Lot: Weddings by the Numbers." *CNN Living.* 9 August 2013. Web. 22 December 2013.

Haydon, John. "The List: Famous Weddings." *The Washington Times.* 23 April 2011. Web. 22 June 2013.

Hicken, Melanie. "Average Wedding Bill in 2012: $28,400." *CNNMoney.* 10 March 2013. Web. 2 January 2014.

Homaday, Ann. Rev. of *27 Dresses,* dir. Anne Fletcher. *Washington Post.* 18 January 2008. Web. 21 January 2014.

Ingraham, Sue. *White Weddings: Romancing Heterosexuality in Popular Culture.* New York: Routledge, 2008. Print.

Italie, Leanne. "*Bridezillas* TV Show Coming to an End." *Huffington Post.* 19 July 2013. Web. 18 September 2013.

"Jeanine and Rochelle." *Bridezillas.* WeTV. Catherine Scheinman, Creator. Season 9, Episode 4. July 2012. Television.

Macy's. Advertisement. *Brides Magazine.* Oct./Nov. 2013: 54-55. Print.

McCracken, Ellen. *Decoding Women's Magazines: From Mademoiselle to Ms.* New York: St. Martin's Press. 1993. Print.

Otnes, Cele C., and Elizabeth H. Pleck. *Cinderella Dreams: The Allure of the Lavish Wedding.* Berkeley: U of CA Press. 2003. Print.

Pozner, Jennifer L. *Reality Bites Back: The Troubling Truth about Guilty Pleasure TV.* Berkley: Seal Press, 2010. Print.

Rothman, Ellen K. *Hands and Hearts: A History of Courtship in America.* New York: Basic Books, Inc. 1984. Print.

"Royal Wedding 2011: Top 8 Moments of William and Catherine's Big Day." *ABC Online.* Web. 13 June 2013.

Sex and the City: The Movie. Dir. Michael Patrick King. Perf. Sarah Jessica Parker, Kim Cattrall, Kristin Davis, and Cynthia Nixon. Warner Brothers, 2008. DVD.

Spender, Dale, ed. *Weddings and Wives.* Penguin Books Australia. 1994. Print.

Stephens, Rebecca. "Socially Soothing Stories? Gender, Race, and Class in TLC's *A Wedding Story* and *A Baby Story. Understanding Reality Television.* Eds. Su Holmes and Deborah Jermyn. London: Routledge, 2004. 191-210. Print.

"Wedding Statistics, Industry Reports and Wedding Trends. *The Wedding Report.* 18 June 2013. Web. 28 December 2013.

Wignall, Alice. "Can a Feminist Really Love *Sex and the City?*" Rev. of *Sex and the City,* Dir. Michael Patrick King. *The Guardian.* 15 April 2008. Web. 21 January 2014.

Chapter Eight

Epideictic Rhetoric in *Jezebel's* Breastfeeding Blogs: The Battle for Normalcy

Kristi McDuffie

Breastfeeding in Public Discourse

Breastfeeding rhetoric has proliferated in recent public discourse. In February 2012, Facebook took down pictures of women breastfeeding. In March, Air National Guard members Terran Echegoyen-McCabe and Christina Luna were reprimanded by the Washington Air National Guard for being photographed while breastfeeding their children in uniform. *Time* magazine featured a picture of attachment parent Jamie Lynne Grumet nursing her three-year-old son in May. In August, Professor Adrienne Pine caused a controversy by breastfeeding her sick daughter during the first day of class (Karin). The public has had extremely strong reactions to such events; at the same time that some people criticized Echegoyen-McCabe and Luna for their actions, others applauded them. Breastfeeding rhetoric elicits some of the strongest praise and blame rhetoric in contemporary U.S. public discourses. One particular online women's blog, *Jezebel,* demonstrates the variation and strength of breastfeeding rhetoric in its scope and tone of its posts.

By looking at the praise and blame rhetoric, or what Aristotle calls epideictic rhetoric, of breastfeeding discourse in *Jezebel,* this chapter finds that this rhetoric encompasses constant arguments for what should be normative about breastfeeding. Following Judy Segal's application of epideictic rhetoric to medical discourses and utilizing Lennard Davis's concept of normalcy, this chapter analyzes breastfeeding rhetoric as a site of contention about normalcy regarding women's bodies, behaviors, and values. Ultimately, this analysis determines that the use of epideictic rhetoric, as well as corresponding rhetoric that argues for any behavior to be normative in women's lives, is not supportive of women; instead, breastfeeding rhetoric should refrain from arguing for any particular norm and embrace diversity in women's bodies and women's lives.

My Story

It has become common practice for researchers to disclose their subjectivities related to their work, so this section briefly describes the impetus for this project. A few months after my first son was born, I attended a women's studies symposium at my university. A sociology graduate student presented on her study of Latina immigrant women's views on breastfeeding. The study was based on three major premises: that breastfeeding was a healthy practice, that not breastfeeding was an unhealthy practice, and that Latina immigrant women have lower rates of breastfeeding the longer they are in the U.S. Her findings included research participants commenting on how American women were lazy and not good mothers because of their lower breastfeeding rates. I was extremely upset by these premises. Three months earlier I had birthed my first son, and he had an unexpected complication when he was born. Although I had very much wanted to breastfeed, in the whirlwind of blood transfusions and sleeping in the NICU while recovering from labor, I tried but failed to breastfeed or pump while in the hospital. My milk had not only come in, but it had also gone away by the time we brought our son home. At the encouragement of my pediatrician's lactation consultant, I continued to try, and pumped dry for three weeks, crying every day, until I finally gave up and gave my son formula.

During that women's symposium, I shot my hand up at the beginning of the Q&A and advised that the presenter reconsider a binary that labels women who are not breastfeeding as bad mothers. Her advisor came to her defense by arguing that it is not a researcher's job to problematize participants' responses, and an audience member argued that women can pump at work. But I insisted that there are multiple reasons why women do not breastfeed and that it *is* the job of the researcher to problematize the premises of her study.

Looking back, I know that my strong reaction was fueled by how pro-breastfeeding rhetoric made me feel like a bad mother because I did not ultimately breastfeed. These experiences, along with the birth of my second son, who also had a NICU stay and who also did not breastfeed after being bottle-fed for ten days, led me to severely question the breastfeeding rhetoric that circulates in our society. "Breast is best" has become commonplace in my discourse communities and in public discourses, but because I felt so misled by this rhetoric, I wanted to investigate what a rhetorical analysis might reveal about these discourses. It is certainly kairotic that my own personal experiences occurred during an animated public dialogue about breastfeeding, women's bodies, and "good" mothers.

Research Methodology

My methodology for this rhetorical analysis is influenced by two primary theories: Judy Segal's application of Aristotle's theory of epideictic rhetoric, which she uses to study medical discourses, and Lennard Davis's concept of "normalcy," which he uses to interrogate disability. In *Health and the Rhetoric of Medicine*, Segal uses rhetorical criticism to study medical discourses. Building upon neo-Aristotelian rhetorical theory (and greatly influenced by Edwin Black, Kenneth Burke, and others), Segal defines rhetorical criticism as "an intentionally underspecified procedure, with certain characteristic interests, for the study of persuasive elements, in a wide range of texts, especially in the realm of social action or public discourse" (10). Rhetorical inquiry is greatly influenced by ideological critique and is linked to rhetorical criticism as social action. Similarly, this chapter engages with rhetoric not only to understand social human actions, but also to influence those actions; this approach to rhetoric draws on Roderick Hart's espousal: "I am a critic, ultimately, because I am a citizen" (qtd. in Segal 16).

Segal uses epideictic rhetoric as a form of invention for analyzing pathologies, or illness narratives. She outlines Aristotle's three types of rhetoric as follows:

> Aristotle identifies three occasions for rhetoric: deliberative, forensic, and epideictic. Deliberative rhetoric is speechmaking directed at the future...; its business is exhortation and dissuasion, and its exemplary genre is the political speech. Forensic rhetoric is speechmaking trained on the past; its business is accusation and defense, and its exemplary genre is the advocate's summation in a court of law. Epideictic rhetoric is the rhetoric of the present; its business...is praise and blame, and its exemplary genre is the funeral oration. (61)

Segal continues that epideictic rhetoric is particularly useful to study culture:

> Epideictic rhetoric is a culture's most telling rhetoric, because, in general, we praise people for embodying what we value, and we blame them for embodying what we deplore. We discover what people's values are by

listening to the eulogies they have composed or by reading the letters of recommendation they have written. (61)

Because of this connection to culture, Segal applies epideictic rhetoric to pathologies. She asks, "What are we doing when we compose and when we study personal narratives of illness? What is it that the work itself honors? What values does the work itself praise?" (62). Similarly, breastfeeding rhetoric is a telling representation of the values in our culture about women's bodies and motherhood. This essay adds to Segal's methodology in that it not only looks for what the rhetoric reveals about our values, but it also analyzes how epideictic rhetoric is used to argue *for* certain cultural values. In this way, breastfeeding rhetoric is a site of negotiation embodying debates about women's bodies, motherhood, feminism, and medicalization. Furthermore, this project focuses on how epideictic rhetoric in breastfeeding discourse is used to argue for normative understandings of women's bodies and motherhood.

In *Enforcing Normalcy,* Davis explains that the concept of normalcy informs how we understand disability. His second chapter details how the concept of normalcy was socially constructed through the rise of statistics, which created the "norm" and the "average" (27). The design of the statistical bell curve is what led to the concept of the "abnormal" or "deviant":

> The concept of a norm, unlike that of an ideal, implies that the majority of the population must or should somehow be part of the norm. The norm pins down that majority of the population that falls under the arch of the standard bell-shaped curve....Any bell curve will always have at its extremities those characteristics that deviate from the norm. So, with the concept of the norm comes the concept of deviations or extremes. When we think of bodies, in a society where the concept of the norm is operative, then people with disabilities will be thought of as deviates. (29)

In this way, statistics enable eugenics, which attempted to "norm" the population. Out of this historical, cultural context has emerged a "hegemony of normalcy" that "permeates our contemporary life" (Davis 49). As a result, we are always situating ourselves in relation to the norm; whether we want to be or whether we even realize it, "[e]ach of us endeavors to be normal or else deliberately tries to avoid that label" (Davis 23). Although being unable to breastfeed is not usually considered a disability, not breastfeeding is often treated as undesired or abnormal in public discourses. But this is not always true—sometimes breastfeeding is treated as the deviation from formula feeding. Which practice should be constituted as the norm is often under debate in breastfeeding rhetoric, so

Davis's concept of normalcy is vital to consider with Segal's use of epideictic rhetoric. Epideictic rhetoric is used to argue for normalized understandings of women's breastfeeding practices.

The women's blogazine *Jezebel* is a productive space for a rhetorical analysis of breastfeeding rhetoric because it is a fascinating and influential site of rhetorical production depicting representations of women. This chapter examines several specific blog posts on *Jezebel* about breastfeeding and contextualizes those posts in the larger breastfeeding conversation generally appearing on *Jezebel*. This chapter identifies rhetorical strategies that authors use, often for shaming or praising certain breastfeeding behaviors, to show that the rhetors are arguing for normative practices. Choosing one site of analysis allows for in-depth analysis, but of course *Jezebel* is not representative of U.S. public discourse on breastfeeding at large; it is only one forum for such discourse that is necessarily culturally contextualized according to race, class, gender, sexuality, and disability.

Brief History of Breastfeeding and Breastfeeding Rhetoric Research

The discourse on breastfeeding found in *Jezebel* emerges from centuries of changing breastfeeding practices and corresponding rhetoric. Bernice Hausman explains that for most of history, women nursed their own infants (7). Wetnursing was common in particular places, such as France in the 17th century, but it was rare for infants to be fed in another manner. For example, infants did not thrive on cow's milk prior to refrigeration (Hausman 7). Refrigeration, along with sanitary water supplies, introduced viable infant feeding alternatives (like formula) in the late 19th and 20th centuries, and breastfeeding declined accordingly (Blum 20). The decline was not without challenge, as immigration concerns in the early 20th century led to pro-breastfeeding efforts (Blum 23). However, later in the 20th century, the medicalization of breastfeeding began as physicians took ownership of infant feeding and breastfeeding resumed its decline (Blum 29). Modern science encouraged mothers, and particularly white, middle-class mothers, to "turn to bottles and formula by the prestige and authoritative weight of modern science, the growing confidence in artificial products, and the declining confidence in breastmilk" (Blum 29-30). This medicalization was linked to the medicalization of birthing practices, as hospital birthing increased during this time period, "[stripping] women of control and [subjecting] them to potentially harmful technological interventions" (Blum 30). The medicalization of breastfeeding also brought increased surveillance, emphasis on cleanliness, and prominence of schedules and, correspondingly, the concept of low milk supply. Because of these factors, by the mid-20th century, breastfeeding was down to about forty percent (Blum 37). Furthermore, this medicalization was intensely racialized. Hausman explains that in the early 20th century,

> Advocates promoted rationalized breastfeeding that mandated scheduled feedings in the context of exclusive nursing for six to nine months; these same advocates criticized foreign, working-class, and nonwhite mothers for irrational breastfeeding that cohered with family or ethnic traditions and that allowed feeding on demand and supplementation with table scraps or other adult foods. (12)

Because of how "strongly entrenched" these factors became (Hausman 12), breastfeeding rates remained relatively low throughout the rest of the 1900s.

As Hausman demonstrates throughout the rest of her monograph, *Mother's Milk*, the tensions embedded in this medicalization model of breastfeeding have created incredibly mixed messages for mothers today. The medical community touts the benefits of breastfeeding while simultaneously insisting on feeding schedules, measuring quantity, and other practices that can impede successful breastfeeding (Hausman 23). The current American Academy of Pediatrics recommendation is that "human milk is superior to infant formula" for the first year of life (Blum 45). But despite this claim, formula is nonetheless a safe alternative that enables infants to thrive (Blum 49), and "[b]ottlefeeding is the normative model for infant feeding, in terms of how infant feeding is approached in routine pediatric practice" (Hausman 23). In addition, formula is readily available in hospitals and is often used to supplement feeding for infants before the mothers' milk comes in, although these practices have recently come under scrutiny (Breslaw). La Leche League actually emerged in response to this deprivation of women's agency brought on by the medicalization model. Blum explains that La Leche League developed out of Catholic-based parent groups who advocated for natural childbirth and breastfeeding (Blum 37).

Another detriment to breastfeeding was women working. This, too, is a tension that women today struggle to negotiate. The maternal model of breastfeeding, which advocates that breastfeeding be seen as a *dyad,* or both mother and infant together, rather than seeing breast milk solely as a product (Hausman 16), is difficult to sustain for working mothers.

These conflicts about breastfeeding in general result in conflicts about breastfeeding within scholarship as well. Breastfeeding has been investigated in numerous fields, with a few works focusing specifically on the rhetoric of breastfeeding. Joan Wolf analyzed the breastfeeding rhetoric of the 2004 National Breastfeeding Awareness Campaign (NBAC). The campaign used risk rhetoric to encourage people to breastfeed. For example, one Public Service Announcement showed images of pregnant women riding mechanical bulls with the comment: "You'd never take risks before your baby is born. Why start after?" Wolf critiques this appeal to fear as lacking sufficient evidence to justify this rhetoric of risk. The spurious analogies make formula feeding seem dangerous, which Wolf finds particularly unethical given a lack of compelling scientific evidence on the risks of not breastfeeding (600). Furthermore, the NBAC exploited "deep-seated normative assumptions about the responsibility that mothers have to protect their babies and children from harm" (Wolf 600-601). Wolf's analysis demonstrates that a rhetoric of fear was used, perhaps unsuccessfully, to take advantage of normative conceptions of motherhood and to argue for breastfeeding as the "safe," normative method of breastfeeding.

Another scholar investigating breastfeeding rhetoric is May Friedman, who finds that breastfeeding advocacy is not necessarily feminist. She critiques several facets of breastfeeding and its accompanying rhetoric, including the reduction of "maternal agency" in favor of children, the guilt invoked by working-class mothers who cannot sustain breastfeeding, the unequal gender roles created between mothers and fathers due to breastfeeding, and the imperative to not only breastfeed, but to "derive pleasure" from it (32). Friedman considers these facets of breastfeeding promotion to be at odds with feminism, which is about women's independence and individualism, and argues for a more feminist rhetoric of choice in breastfeeding discourse.

When put into conversation, what Hausman, Blum, Wolf, Friedman, and other scholars demonstrate is that there is an overarching disagreement on what should be "normal" about breastfeeding. Many feminist scholars argue against the maternal model that prioritizes breastfeeding and puts women's needs below their children's. But other scholars, like Hausman, argue that it *is* feminist to encourage breastfeeding because of the biomedical benefits of breastfeeding (Hausman 6). This argument is evident in public discourses overall. As the rhetorical analysis of the *Jezebel* posts will demonstrate, many women *feel* that breastfeeding is the norm in our society. I felt this way, too, while pregnant and still feel this way now because most of the mothers I know breastfeed.

However, if breastfeeding advocacy has been successful in establishing a perception that breastfeeding is normative in contemporary U.S. society, there remains a large disconnect between breastfeeding rhetoric and breastfeeding rates. The American Academy of Pediatrics recommends that infants be breastfed exclusively for the first six months and continued for at least the first year, and initiatives such as the National Breastfeeding Awareness and the Healthy People 2010 campaigns seek to increase breastfeeding rates. But rates continue to be much lower than desired. The National Immunization Survey of 2004-2008 finds that rates are 72.4% at initiation, 41.7% at six months, and 21.0% at one year (CDC). These rates, like breastfeeding rhetoric itself, are classed and raced. The same report details much lower rates for African Americans (54.4%, 26.6%, and 11.7%, respectively), higher rates for college graduates (85.4%, 51.7%, and 25.5%, respectively), and higher rates for mothers over thirty (77.5%, 48.5%, and 25.4%, respectively). Thus, breastfeeding rhetoric that constructs breastfeeding as normative is not supported with statistics that show that breastfeeding, while most practiced by educated white women over thirty, is not the main method of infant feeding in the U.S.

These low rates create an imperative for strong breastfeeding advocacy, and this advocacy creates pressure to breastfeed; many women deem such strong pressure to be vindictive and burdening to women, rather than supportive. These conflicts lead to rhetoric that debates what should be normative about breastfeeding, as is evident in numerous posts on breastfeeding in *Jezebel.*

Analysis

Jezebel began in 2007 as a feminist break-out from the blogazine *Gawker.* Attaining 200,000 visits per day, it is a self-purported "general interest women's website" (Coen) with the slogan "Celebrity, Sex, Fashion for Women." Despite the self-advertising as a women's online magazine focusing on fashion and celebrity gossip, the website is a notable forum for media criticism. In addition to discussing superficial topics, it also covers serious issues like politics and media representations of women. Yet, because it is not a traditional news outlet beholden to an ideal of objectivity, the blogazine can use epideictic rhetoric and its related rhetorical strategies overtly as a means of cultural critique.

Jezebel employs rhetoric of praise and blame in many of its posts, such as in headlines like "Racist *Hunger Games* Fans Are Very Disappointed" (Stewart), "10 Reasons Why Ryan Lochte Is America's Sexiest Douchebag" (Ryan, "10 Reasons Why"), and "A Girl's Guide To Treating Symptoms Of Unwanted Pregnancies" (Morrissey, "A Girl's Guide"). *Jezebel* has even gotten criticized for its epideictic rhetoric. For example, in 2010, it caused a stir by calling Comedy Central's *The Daily Show* sexist based on reports from former female writers and correspondents who claimed the environment was sexist (Mascia). This strong rhetoric is evident in its breastfeeding articles as well.

Jezebel publishes pieces on breastfeeding as part of its "Breast Intentions" and "Breastfeeding" categories. These articles are part of a more general focus on women's bodies, like pregnancy, and a particular focus on women's breasts, from implants to breast cancer. The increase in public discourse about breastfeeding recently has led to a corresponding increase in posts about breastfeeding on *Jezebel*. A number of these posts are short reports on breastfeeding issues in the news, although even these articles are opinionated. For example, the short report on a Luvs diaper commercial in October 2012 opines that it is "pretty cool" to "make breastfeeding look like a totally okay and maybe even important thing to do" ("Public"). The commercial shows two scenarios: first, a mother struggles to cover up while breastfeeding in a restaurant and the words "First Kid" appear onscreen. Then, the same mother sits calmly and confidently breastfeeding without a cover and the words "Second Kid" appear. The commercial, as well as the *Jezebel* coverage of it, suggests that women should feel confident breastfeeding in public.

In the longer pieces, ranging from 250 to 900 words, epideictic rhetoric is overt. There is praise for breastfeeding advocacy efforts, such as "Government Cracks Down On Employers Who Don't Accommodate Breastfeeding Moms" (Hartmann), alongside blame for those not supporting breastfeeding, such as "We're Seriously Debating Whether It's Okay for Military Moms to Breastfeed While in Uniform?" (Ryan, "We're Seriously Debating"). Published alongside these pro-breastfeeding posts is blame for breastfeeding advocacy, such as "The Pressure to Breastfeed Is Getting Out of Hand" (Morrissey, "The Pressure to Breastfeed") and "Breastfeeding Gestapo Moves to Ban Free Formula Samples from Hospitals" (Morrissey, "Breastfeeding Gestapo"). To demonstrate how these posts include epideictic rhetoric that displays cultural values, this chapter analyzes several selections in detail.

In "Sorry—You Can't Guilt Trip Me About Bottle Feeding My Kids," Sarah Fister Gale argues that "[b]ottle-feeding my babies was one of the best parenting decisions I ever made." Her claim is a bold response to the pressure to breastfeed, which was put upon her by friends while she was pregnant and lactation consultants after she gave birth. The rhetoric of blame is most clearly visible through her pejorative language. Gale describes friends and lactation "zealots" as a "caterwauling mob" on a "righteous path." The lactation consultants are depicted as aggressive and ridiculous. A consultant "barged" into her room and was a "towering menace of a woman with plasticky blond hair" and "garish lipstick." Later, that same "bully" "glared" at her. Having told the doctor that she was going to bottle-feed her second child, she writes that he had "contempt in his voice" and "rolled his eyes and dismissed [her]" (Gale). Gale's hyperbolic strategy of describing these events demonstrates the judgment and blame she felt during these experiences.

Hyperbole occurs throughout this post. For example, Gale says that a lactation consultant told her, "[Your baby] will almost certainly die of typhus, or swine flu, or some dastardly childhood disease that breast milk can absolutely prevent" and that "formula is made from nicotine and tequila and mashed up dung beetles." Gale follows up with "Okay, she didn't actually say any of that, but she insinuated it." Other examples of hyperbole are not confessed, such as when Gale describes how her children were healthy, happy babies. She writes, "Except for the occasional runny nose or ear infection, they survived babyhood without a single bout of measles, or croup, or bubonic plague" (Gale). Since the bubonic plague is not a concern in 21st century America, including it as an example makes the breastfeeding advocate look ridiculous. The combination of the pejorative language and hyperbole situates Gale as a reasonable person and the breastfeeding advocates as unreasonable and absurd. Although this article is written in response to the shame and guilt of pro-breastfeeding rhetoric, it, too, participates in an epideictic tradition by utilizing praise and blame techniques.

The effect of Gale's rhetoric is to argue for a revised normative definition of a "good" mother. In contrast to the pro-breastfeeding rhetoric's technique of establishing breastfeeding as a must for good mothering, Gale's rhetorical strategies establish her as a good mother for making reasonable decisions in the best interest of her children, herself, and her family. (Usually pro-breastfeeding rhetoric is only focused on the benefits for the children.) Gale also establishes herself as a feminist for including her needs in addition to those of her children and for recognizing that attending to her needs *is* in the best interest of her children. This revisionary rhetoric might be becoming more common as it is also evident in Chris Kornelis's Oct. 31st, 2012 article in *The Atlantic* titled "A Father's Case Against Breastfeeding: It May Be the Healthiest Choice For a Baby...But Not Necessarily For Sleep-deprived Parents." Overall, Gale also establishes that the pressure to breastfeed is normative in our public and private discourses and argues for a different norm that values and respects formula feeding.

Even more overt epideictic rhetoric can be found in a December 2012 post called "Fuck You, Breastfeeding" by Tracie Egan Morrissey. This post was part of "Fuck You Week" on *Jezebel,* which was *"Jezebel's* first annual week of desperate emotional cleansing and unhinged psychic purging" (Morrissey, "Fuck You"). To be fair, then, the purpose of that week of posts was to be inflammatory; to that end, the posts ranged from serious topics like "Fuck You, Cancer" and "Fuck You, Guns" to lighter topics such as "Fuck You, Other People's Children" and "Fuck You, GChat." Nonetheless, Morrissey's rhetoric is still strong: "Breastfeeding can fuck off, right now" (Morrissey, "Fuck You"). Morrissey's point overall is to protest the pressure that made her feel like she had to breastfeed, and keep breastfeeding, despite severe pain and even during "the time [her] left nipple fell off" (Morrissey, "Fuck You"). Morrissey makes several points that contribute to breastfeeding discussions; to begin, she illustrates the kind of physical pain that is not often brought up in breastfeeding rhetoric and demonstrates that there is little support to help women get through that pain. She also goes against the norm of how infatuated new mothers often are of their babies by describing how much she resented her daughter because of the pain. Morrissey also problematizes the notion that fathers can be helpful because only women are able to give birth and breastfeed. Finally, she makes a claim that all women, not just adoptive parents or women who have low milk supplies, should be able to use formula without being criticized.

Morrissey's point is to challenge many of the normative assumptions about breastfeeding, and most notably, that it is supposed to be pleasurable for the mother. While many women would certainly appreciate her honestly, others would surely be offended. Morrissey's sharp rhetoric of blame is indicting, accusatory, and petulant. She uses pejorative and hyperbolic language, including phrases such as "lactivist cunts," and "Mind your own tits" (Morrissey, "Fuck You"). Rather than writing that fathers are unable to do as much work as mothers, she calls them sperm donors:

> Colloquially, 'mothering' implies nurturing. 'Fathering' implies insemination. Because—while my tits were falling off and my back was fucked up from pregnancy-induced scoliosis and my healing C-section incision made me afraid to sneeze—that was my husband's sole physical contribution in this whole thing: a sloppy pullout. (Morrissey, "Fuck You")

Similarly, Morrissey does not write that all women should have the freedom of choice to use formula; she criticizes some women as getting a "pass" from the shunning if they are adoptive parents or unable to provide sufficient milk. She continues, "Formula is for anyone who fucking wants it. It doesn't matter what their reasons are. Maybe they're in pain, maybe they're tired, maybe they think nursing bras are ugly, maybe they want to do drugs—it doesn't fucking matter" (Morrissey, "Fuck You"). Although Morrissey is advocating for women's choice, the aim is undercut by her ableist rhetoric that shames women who are unable to breastfeed in favor of women who can, but do not wish to. Overall, then, Morrissey's attempt to rewrite normalizing breastfeeding practices constructs a rhetoric of blame, rather than valuing a diversity of women's bodies and experiences.

A post that is more successful in challenging unproductive normative representations of breastfeeding is one that criticizes, rather than engages in, a rhetoric of blame. In "Similac Recall: Breastfeeders, Hold the Sanctimony," Maria Mora responds to breastfeeding advocacy that appeared in response to a Similac formula recall in 2010. After the event, people tweeted that "breast milk doesn't get recalled" (Mora). Mora quickly establishes her ethos to those who value breastfeeding by claiming that she is "all for promoting the benefits of breastfeeding" and that her "boys never had formula" (Mora). But she complicates this position by noting the difficulty of breastfeeding—she describes having clogged ducts, pumping in closets, and dieting when breast milk gave her son rashes (Mora). She then notes that, because of the difficulties accompanying breastfeeding, she knows how much breast-is-best rhetoric can be hurtful. She analogizes formula to allergy medicine, which works when it has to.

As she discusses breastfeeding, Mora does not praise those who do breastfeed, nor does she blame those who do not. Her discussion is more nuanced and complicated in that she makes space for both people who do and people who do not breastfeed, without judging their decisions. She writes, "Life happens. Formula happens. You know who formula happens to, in particular? Women who can't breastfeed. Fathers caring for babies on their own. Adoptive parents caring for babies" (Mora). Because of this understanding, Mora is critical of people who wrote gloating comments about breastfeeding in response to the Similac recall: "You know what those parents don't want to read? Shitty, spiteful comments about how 'well if you were breastfeeding, you wouldn't have to worry about feeding your kid beetle parts'" (Mora). She is, in essence, condemning the epideictic rhetoric that creates a culture of praise and blame about breastfeeding. Thus, in avoiding epideictic rhetoric about breastfeeding, Mora abstains from the normalizing game. She is advocating support for all parents and all parenting decisions without arguing for any normalized conception of motherhood. Ultimately, Mora's post demonstrates the possibilities for breastfeeding discourse that makes space for a multitude of women's bodies, lives, and decisions, without prioritizing any particular practices in a way that continues to construct norms that can never work for all women.

Conclusion

Although various blog posts on *Jezebel* conflict about how much or even whether to breastfeed, many of the posts debate normative behaviors of "good" mothers. Using epideictic rhetoric, pro-breastfeeding and pro-formula feeding advocates present their arguments in relation to the other and claim a marginalized subjectivity in order to argue that their position should be the new norm. Ultimately, this analysis suggests that discourses surrounding infant feeding would be the most productive if they depicted the variation and multiplicity of women's bodies and women's lives without arguing for any particular norm. Arguing for normalcy only further marginalizes and produces guilt in particular mothers for specific behaviors, and therefore, altering breastfeeding rhetoric to be more accepting and understanding of a variety of behaviors and choices is the best way to truly support women.

Works Cited

Blum, Linda M. *At the Breast: Ideologies of Breastfeeding and Motherhood in the Contemporary United States.* Boston: Beacon Press, 1999. Print.

Breslaw, Anna. "In Two Days Mayor Bloomberg Will Make You Put Your Nipple In Your Kid's Mouth." 1 Sept. 2012. *Jezebel.com* Web. 4 Nov. 2012.

Centers for Disease Control and Prevention (CDC). "Racial and Ethnic Differences in Breastfeeding Initiation and Duration, by State—National Immunization Survey, United States, 2004–2008." *Morbidity and Mortality Weekly Report* 59.11 (2010): 327-334. Web. 9 Nov. 2012.

Coen, Jennifer. Interview Clip. *Jezebel.com.* Web. 6 Nov. 2012.

Davis, Lennard J. "Constructing Normalcy." *Enforcing Normalcy: Disability, Deafness, and the Body.* London: Verso, 1995. 23-49. Print.

Friedman, May. "For Whom is Breast Best? Thoughts on Breastfeeding, Feminism and Ambivalence." *Journal of the Association for Research on Mothering* 11.1 (2009): 26-35. Print.

Gale, Sarah Fister. "Sorry—You Can't Guilt Trip Me About Bottle Feeding My Kids." *Jezebel* 15 Aug. 2012. *Jezebel.com.* Web. 15 Aug. 2012.

Hartman, Margaret. "Government Cracks Down On Employers Who Don't Accommodate Breastfeeding Moms." 4 Jan. 2012. *Jezebel.com*. Web. 5 Jun. 2013.

Hausman, Bernice L. *Mother's Milk: Breastfeeding Controversies in American Culture*. New York: Routledge, 2003. Print.

Karin, Marcy. "Reasonable Break Time Provided Amidst the Breastfeeding Media Craze." *Huffington Post Parents*. 24 Oct. 2012. Web. 30 Oct. 2012.

Kornelis, Chris. "A Father's Case Against Breast-Feeding." *The Atlantic* 31 Oct. 2012. Web. 9 Nov. 2012.

Mascia, Jennifer. "A Web Site That's Not Afraid to Pick a Fight." *The New York Times*. 11 Jul. 2010. *nytimes.com*. Web. 5 Nov. 2012.

Mora, Maria. "Similac Recall: Breastfeeders, Hold the Sanctimony." 23 Sept. 2010. *Jezebel.com* Web. 8 Mar. 2013.

Morrissey, Tracie Egan. "A Girl's Guide to Treating Symptoms of Unwanted Pregnancies." 30 Dec. 2012. *Jezebel.com*. Web. 5 Jun. 2013.

—. "Breastfeeding Gestapo Moves to Ban Free Formula Samples from Hospitals." 11 Apr. 2012. *Jezebel.com*. Web. 5 Jun. 2013.

—. "Fuck You, Breastfeeding." 17 Dec. 2012. *Jezebel.com*. Web. 8 Mar. 2013.

—. "The Pressure to Breastfeed Is Getting Out of Hand." 7 Aug. 2012. *Jezebel.com*. Web. 5 Jun. 2013.

"Public Breastfeeding is Awesome, Says Luvs." *Jezebel.com* 1 Oct. 2012. Web. 2 Nov. 2012.

Ryan, Erin Gloria. "10 Reasons Why Ryan Lochte Is America's Sexiest Douchebag." 2 Aug. 2012. *Jezebel.com*. Web. 5 Jun. 2013.

—. "We're Seriously Debating Whether It's Okay for Military Moms to Breastfeed While in Uniform?" 31 May 2012. *Jezebel.com*. Web. 5 Jun. 2013.

Segal, Judy Z. *Health and the Rhetoric of Medicine*. Carbondale, IL: Southern Illinois UP, 2005. Print.

Stewart, Dodai. "Racist Hunger Games Fans Are Very Disappointed." 26 Mar. 2012. *Jezebel.com*. Web. 5 Jun. 2013.

Wolf, Joan B. "Is Breast Really Best? Risk and Total Motherhood in the National Breastfeeding Awareness Campaign." *Journal of Health Politics, Policy and Law* 32.4 (2007): 595-636. Print.

CHAPTER NINE

THE FOREVER INDEBTED BODY: LIFE WITHOUT PAROLE

ADRIENNE BLISS

"Every time I look up at stacked coils of glistening razor wire atop fences around me, for example, I am being told, DON'T TRY ANYTHING – YOUR [sic] SURROUNDED! Fear is reinforced by the redundancy of steel gates and bars that warn THERE IS NO WAY OUT! Unnecessary strip-searches and pat-downs that are repeated obsessively are actually reminders: AT ANY TIME WE CAN DO ANYTHING WE WANT WITH YOU!" (Hassine 7)

According to the Bureau of Justice Statistics report, *Correctional Population in the United States, 2011,* as of December 2012, the incarcerated population for both state and federal facilities was 1,598,780. Correspondingly, the Bureau's *Prisoners in 2011* reports that the "imprisonment rate was 492 inmates per 100,000 U.S. residents in 2011" (U.S. Dept of Justice). Both of these numbers have decreased for the second year in a row; however, the United States still has the highest incarceration rate in the world and remains one of few nations in the world to impose the sentence "life without the possibility of parole" (LWOP) on adults.[1]

Since the 18th century American society has increasingly hidden the world of the prison from public view. Moving from a perspective that included a public concept of punishment to a punitive private setting,

---

[1] The offenses eligible for LWOP sentencing include murder, kidnapping, sexual assault/rape, armed robbery, felony murder, and drug offences: for repeat offenders, an array of felonies can trigger LWOP under habitual offender sentencing (Abramsky; Cunningham and Sorensen; Leigey 11). Lifers include battered women, the mentally ill, juveniles, those serving accountability offenses (felony murder), property offenders, and prisoners sentenced under the three strikes policy (Mauer, King, and Young).

American society has not had to view the outcomes of the judicial system when it led to imprisonment. This has perpetuated a secrecy that has allowed for the exploitation and degradation of both inmates and the people who work in the prison industry. There has also arisen an increase in the writing about this world by prisoners, along with the study of prison writing. Alongside academic research in criminology, psychology, and sociology are prisoners' essays, short stories, plays, poetry, and novels, all of which are increasingly available and anthologized. Prison literature and its study have been growing in political and academic settings since the late 20th century, covering a wide range of genres, academic and non-academic. Using the prisoner accounts in *Life without Parole: Living and Dying in Prison Today* by Victor Hassine and *A Woman Doing Life: Notes from a Women's Prison* by Erin George, along with other prison literature, this chapter provides insight into the creation of the forever-indebted body of the LWOP prisoner.

The societal cost to the U.S., ethically and financially, of LWOP is significant.[2] On a practical basis it is leading to an increasingly aging and costly prison population. However, in terms of ethics, the question for a prisoner facing a life sentence is this: how does one maintain a sense of identity when imprisoned with no chance of ever leaving, or as the prisoners refer to it, death by incarceration. Maintenance of one's identity becomes vital. Although some prisoners may adapt to living in ongoing emotional and mental deprivation as well as fear of physical safety, this level of deprivation and hyper-vigilance can lead to emotional or psychological problems for many prisoners. Therefore, writing has become a tool of hope and resistance for some prisoners. The writings of these women and men are receiving growing recognition and publication as their talent is acknowledged by the literary world and also as the American prison system has come under increased public scrutiny.

The story of incarceration includes humiliation, intimidation, and mortification of self as part of the process of arrest, incarceration, adjudication, and imprisonment, all of which are recurring themes in prison writings. Strip searches, becoming a number, wearing prison uniforms, and enduring open hostility and contempt of the legal system all take place within the first days in jail and are repeated when the person is

---

[2] Ironically "Companies like CCA [Corrections Corporation of American] see jail and prison budgets a recession-proof goldmine; every inmate is worth $22,650, the annual per capita cost of incarnation. With 2.3 million convicts in the U.S., the money-making opportunities are extraordinary" (Soering 30). According to Craig Haney, prison industrial complexes "now wield unprecedented political and economic influence in our society" (68).

sent from jail to prison (Irwin and Owen 107-108; Hassine, George, Goffman 14-48). Regimentation through clothing, for instance, is one of the more effective ways to eliminate agency and the person's unique physical appearance. This is particularly devastating to women as western culture places a strong emphasis on a woman's physical appearance. This chapter explores, among other things, how these prisoners' texts are "framed" in a manner similar to captivity or slave narratives by a socially acceptable voice providing legitimacy and witness. As Robin Riley-Fast claims of slave narratives, "the sponsors commonly testify to the truth of the narrative and the good character of the narrator; if identified as editors, they affirm the slave's own writing of her or his own story" (5). There is another layer of significance to this practice due to the disproportionate number of African Americans and Hispanics in prison serving LWOP. As of 2008, nationally 66.4% of "lifers" are non-white (Nellis and King 3, 11-13). Therefore, the practice of creating a legitimized public forum for minorities grows, as many of the voices coming out of prison are Hispanic or African American.[3]

Framing Narratives

Prison narratives, fiction and non-fiction, are a unique category of literature in part due to the challenge of determining their reality. Though this statement can be made of other types of literature as well, the uniqueness of prison stories is that this is a world the public does not have unlimited access to, so it cannot judge the veracity of the claims made by prisoners or administrators. Nor is this a world the average American wants to understand. Tiffany Lopez points out:

> To speak about prison narratives is also to speak about violence and trauma. Like writings about trauma, prison narratives are characterized by fragmentation and the urgent struggle to speak of experiences formerly perceived as taboo, unspeakable, or otherwise resistant to story. (64)

---

[3] According to Margaret Leigey: "The typical LWOP inmate is male, non-white, and middle-aged and had been incarcerated at least once before serving the present sentence. He has served about 11 years of the LWOP sentence, which he received following a conviction for murder, or manslaughter. Although a much smaller group, the typical female LWOP inmate mirrors her male counterpart in mean age, time served, offense and the overrepresentation of inmates of color. However, it is interesting to note that female LWOP inmates were more likely to be first-time inmates compared with their male counterparts" (10).

As is the case with trauma and slave narratives, the reader of prison literature is required to act as witness and provide validation of the author's existence and humanity. This is said not to lessen the reality or impact of the crimes that have been committed or the need for prisons, but to recognize that having a sentence of LWOP does not automatically make a prisoner inhuman.

The introduction or framing of a prison or slave narrative by a legitimizing voice is common in literature. The framing of these texts, though, can seem to increase the individual's indebtedness. As Riley-Fast notes with reference to slave narratives, "sponsors, while they explicitly share this aim of winning a hearing for the subjects, may actually muffle the slaves' voices, by the very nature of their interventions" and establish a "context for the reading, [and] determine or at least influence the reader's responses" (6). The editorial voice of the introduction can act to set the agenda for the stories to be told as opposed to the authors' words speaking for themselves. It is as if there is an "official" voice telling the reader why this text is acceptable to read. Overall, the framing ranges greatly depending on the editor and purpose of the writing.

Sally Gomaa, writing about slave narratives, points out that "The radical transformation from 'thing' to 'man' was enacted on the abolitionist platform by displaying slaves' bodies in pain" (371). A similar practice takes place in prison writing. The stories describing the suffering and brutality that prisoners face is designed to elicit empathy for the inmate and anger at the prison system, as is evident in Hassine and George's stories. Gomaa further writes of abolitionists that their "sentimentalism treated pain as a prerequisite for a sort of sympathetic activism by assuming that witnessing pain was akin to experiencing it" and the "position exemplifies the abolitionist treatment of pain as visual and of the slave's body as spectacle" in a manner very similar to Foucault's discussion of the condemned body (Gomaa 372-74; Foucault 3-31). Audiences reading prison literature have an analogous voyeuristic experience; the reader is sympathetic but treats the prisoner's body as spectacle. There is an expectation on the audience's part of violence and exploitation when reading this literature. Framing by a legitimizing voice allows the audience to provide witness at a safe distance when reading about prisons and prisoners, and this distance can correspondingly allow readers to further marginalize prisoners (and guards) as "other."

A concern, though, in slave narratives or prison literature is how the framing voice may control the content of the text. Riley-Fast notes that framing in the slave narratives was "most often [a constructed practice] which tended to muffle the protagonist's individual voices" (3). In one book about life in a private prison, *Prison, Inc.*, the author even claims his indebtedness to the authoritative and legitimizing voice of his editor, Thomas J. Bernard (Carceral). Bernard changed the author's name to a pseudonym, K.C. Carceral, and in the text Carceral is referred to as Anonymous Number Inmate for the author's safety. This leaves the prisoner without legitimate identity, and readers must rely on Bernard for proof the story is "real." There are, however, different approaches to framing in prison narratives generally dependent on whether they are collected interviews, fiction, ethnographies, poetry, or essays; also, the author and the publisher are, of course, important. Of all of these, the use of ethnography implies the most present and perhaps controlling voice of the narrator, as seen in Hassine and George's work.

Prison fiction is sometimes published without a framing voice, but collections of writings and autobiographies still have an introductory voice in the form of an editor who is often an academic. Bruce Franklin's *Prison Writing in 20th-Century America* and Bell Gale Chevigney's *Doing Time: 25 Years of Prison Writing* are anthologies that provide excellent examples of an editorial presence. Both editors focus on selections of texts versus extensive commentaries on the authors' experiences and ideas. There is an argument to be made that in their position as "gatekeepers," Franklin and Chevigney exercise power in their decisions of what to include, an argument that must be kept in mind with any anthology.

Some books tend to have more of an outside editorial introduction that includes discussion of how the author came to be in prison or social commentary. In Patricia McConnel's book, *Sing Soft, Sing Loud,* the text opens directly to her short stories, though she does write her own "Afterward" that includes a call to action asking readers to get involved in prison reform. John Edgar Wideman's "Introduction" in Mumia Abu-Jamal's *Life from Death Row* provides an example of social commentary in which Wideman discusses the "neo-slave narrative" as a tool of oppression and how "the best slave narratives and prison narratives have always asked profound questions, implicitly and explicitly, about the meaning of a life" (xxxvi). The introduction is more political polemic than a testament to the legitimacy of Abu-Jamal's story, though some might argue that Wideman does provide a radical legitimacy. Wideman allows for Abu-Jamal's voice to be dominant, whereas in the ethnographies edited by Johnson he is directing content and purpose.

Robert Johnson, as editor, has a clear agenda that includes empathizing with the respective authors and expressing indignation at the cruelty of the system. In addition, both prisoners came from middle class backgrounds and earned college degrees, which is far from the norm in prisoners in

general. Johnson is directing the way the narratives are told and progress.
His editorial presence is particularly evident in George's book, where he
introduces each chapter by telling the audience exactly what is in the
chapter, only to have the same information related by George. Johnson
sets each book up in a similar manner in terms of chapter topics, and in
Hassine's text Johnson uses his own poem to start the book. George claims
to have followed Hassine's style, but it seems more of an editorial than an
authorial choice. This variance can be a result of the different genres, but
George and Hassine's stories are clearly constructed narratives. What is
important about these and other formal writings is the credence and
support they provide to other types of prison writing and that they are part
of a chorus of voices seeking recognition. As prisoners' stories,
ethnographies, and collections of interviews have increasingly become part
of academic discourse, these stories have also added to the legitimacy and
visibility of prisoners' writings, fictional and otherwise.

Identity

Erving Goffman's definition of institutionalization claimed prison to
be a place of destruction of individual identity with the potential of
creating either a violent being who has nothing to lose or a prisoner living
in abject despair. As more studies were conducted in the late 20th century,
this outlook became disputed as researchers claimed prisoners experienced
an initial period of depression and/or anger, but this was followed by
adaptation to prison.[4] The truth seems to lie somewhere in between and
perhaps is best found in the writings of the prisoners themselves.
Goffman's work, however, provides a basic framework on which to
understand the experience of prison.

Goffman describes total institutions like prisons as "having an
encompassing tendency symbolized by the barrier to social intercourse
with the outside that is built right into the physical plant" (4). The total
institution is "a place of residence and work where a large number of like-
situated individuals, cut off from the wider society for an appreciable
period of time, together lead an enclosed, formally administered round of
life" (xiii). He illustrates four totalistic features of an inmate's life in a
total institution:

---

[4] See Flanagan, Cunningham and Sorensen, Dobrzanska and Johnson, Haney,
Irwin and Owen, MacKenzie and Goodstein, MacKenzie, Peck, Jervis, Sorensen
and Wrinkle, Wormith, Zamble for additional discussion.

First, all aspects of life are conducted in the same place and under the same single authority. Second, each phase of the member's daily activity will be carried out in the immediate company of a large batch of others, all of whom are treated alike and required to do the same thing together. Third, all phases of the day's activities are tightly scheduled, with one activity leading at a prearranged time into the next, the whole circle of activities being imposed from above through a system of explicit formal rulings and a body of officials. Finally, the contents of the various enforced activities are brought together as parts of a single overall rational plan purportedly designed to fulfill the official aims of the institution. (6)

These features set the stage for the dehumanization that prisons can inflict. The psychological damage inmates experience includes loss of agency and ability to control their destiny. Routinization and restriction create few opportunities to make decisions, thus further decreasing the inmate's agency (Irwin and Owen 98-100; Goffman 23). Endless days of hyperawareness, boredom, and random moments of violence stretch out before a prisoner with LWOP all of which work wear down any sense of individuality and agency.

Goffman illustrates how the admissions process is a "leaving off and a taking on [of identity], with the midpoint marked by physical nakedness" (19). New admissions are forced into a frightening and inhuman world, which begins when personal possessions and names are taken away and continues as they are deloused in a cold shower in view of the guards and forced to submit to a body cavity search. Losing one's identity includes a loss of personal property such as shampoo or even a child's picture. The loss of one's name is more significant, though, than personal possessions, as names define the person in a more essential way through connections to family, friends, and a life outside the prison. All of these events take place with little or no explanation. Fragmentation, chaos, confusion, and unbearable physical living conditions are often themes in prisoners' narratives, which reflect this loss of control and agency.

Hassine illustrates his entrance into Bucks County Jail when relating his arrest and subsequent incarceration, writing:

First came the visual image of captivity: dark, dirty, scarred floors and walls; dusty, dim lighting fixtures dangling from cathedral-high ceilings; shadows from poor lighting that made distant details hard to discern; a drab colorlessness and harshness to everything in sight; the steady flow of faceless strangers pouring in and out of corridor; the constant presence of stern, uniformed police and prison guards and the unkempt, disheveled appearance of uniformed inmates . . . A prison's voice is a cacophony of interminable, tortuous noises layered together at a constant pitch as pervasive as the air: loud, irritating, vulgar, and out of tune, all trapped by prison design and replayed as fragmented echoes throughout the prison. (3)

Hassine goes on to explain how once his paperwork was completed, he "became the official property of the prison staff" (5). Transferred to Philadelphia County Prison at the request of the District Attorney, Hassine realized that "all [staff] performed with such dispatch and indifference that I knew with certainty now that I was nothing more than property – a prisoner of less importance than the paperwork that identified me" (6). Intake begins the process of marking the prisoner as property versus human. The hyperawareness that one must develop to survive begins upon entering jail and follows the prisoner through conviction and to prison. Similarly, George's thoughts as she was transferred to prison were that she

> only hoped that, tempered by the violence and deprivation of the jail, I had managed to find the balance between the self-preservation that was vital for my own safety and the empathy necessary to keep myself human behind prison walls. (25)

Beginning with intake and continuing throughout an inmate's entire sentence is the adherence to the "Chicken-shit" Rules of the institution that can randomly be changed and enforced with different penalties (Irwin and Owen 105-107). Inmates are expected to learn and adhere to the institutional practices of the prison immediately upon arrival, whether or not they are given a copy of these rules. They are also expected to understand the unofficial rules of the inmates' world (Goffman 9, 48-53). Some of these unofficial rules include the following: do not snitch; do not borrow or lend money; do not get in another inmate's business; do not *ever* back down; and do not make eye contact. Hassine writes that at Graterford Prison "the code went something like this: 'don't gamble, don't mess with drugs, don't mess with homosexuals, don't steal, don't borrow or lend, and you might survive'" (97). George also noted: "One thing you should never do in prison is throw someone's time up in her face...knowing that it demands immediate, violent response" (22). Rules, official and otherwise, serve to support "the architecture of fear" that is the prison (Hassine 7). This is a point when the prisoner learns that "Prisons are uniquely designed to instigate fear in so many creative ways that fear has become a kind of language on its own, silently but relentlessly commanding specific inmate conduct and behavior" (Hassine 7).

Due to the hypermasculinity of men's prisons, intake at some point forces prisoners to "prove" themselves; if not, they do their time as a victim or "punk." The ownership of a punk is established when a weak prisoner enters prison and is robbed, conned, raped, or physically beaten by another prisoner or prisoners while offering little or no protest or show of strength. The culture of prison denies and punishes "the show of feeling, especially among men, where notions of manhood equate vulnerability with weakness" (Chevigny 258). Women are also expected to maintain an inviolate attitude and stone face to survive prison sentences. The goal for inmates is to try to present an ostensibly impermeable physical presence despite any physical, emotional, or psychological vulnerability.

Physical safety is always an issue for prisoners, and the prison complex can exploit this fear (Irwin and Owen 112). "The multiple levels by which the prison world intrudes itself into my psyche have frustrated my efforts to initiate any thought or action that is not first filtered through these engines of fear," claims Hassine (12). Whether it is the threat of a search, violence by other prisoners, loss of privileges, being snitched on, or being written up, the inmates' hyperawareness of their surroundings can never drop. Hassine wrote of the toll that hypervigilance took on his psyche, saying "It seems that Graterford, inch for inch the most life-threatening real estate in Pennsylvania, had somehow conditioned me into a violence and fear addict, accustomed to life on red alert" (Hassine 111). The energy and time that fear consumes reduces the focus needed for more creative or abstract thought.

Judith Scheffler analyzed the effects of imprisonment by identifying "scenes," or events, key to the dehumanizing of inmates; these are based on significant moments in prison life that are highly scripted by prison rules to insure that prisoners do not forget their lack of agency and their designation as a number. For example, prisoners are required to submit to a strip search and cavity search before and after a visit even if there is no physical contact. This search reminds the prisoner that he can neither bring nor take anything away from the visit and that the guards can control even his family life.

In the "Visit Scene," Scheffler identifies how women, although they are often primary caregivers, receive fewer visits due to the difficulty other family members or foster parents have in bringing the children to visit. Mothers facing imprisonment "must struggle with a double stereotype, since society sees them as both disreputable women and unfit mothers" (Scheffler 113). Also, there are fewer women's prisons, and thus women are frequently placed in a facility where their family has little or no access. Travel and the cost of travel can be prohibitive to families struggling to pay their bills. George's children went to live with their father's parents in England and she was only able to see them once a year.

Another version of this scene is the "Frustrated Visit Scene" when prison politics and subjective rule enforcement keep a prisoner from seeing his or her visitor. Scott Bunyan argues, "Visitors are made to feel as if they are being put on trial, found guilty, and effectively condemned for wishing to visit their loved ones" (183). Family members and other visitors must go through a metal detector, pat down, and possibly a drug detector. They can be turned away based on inappropriate clothing, or detained by a guard due to "attitude," which would result in their visit time being reduced. The process of visitation is designed to control and denigrate the prisoner and the visitor, as seen in Judee Norton's *Norton #59900*, when her son is harassed for his attitude, or in John Wideman's *Brothers and Keepers*, when Wideman relates the indignity suffered by visiting family members when body searched, questioned, and sometimes delayed. The prison system has effectively learned how to spread its humiliation to families as well as inmates. Visitors are considered suspect by their association with the prisoner, which causes feelings of guilt and shame in the prisoner and can lead to the inmate requesting that the family no longer visit. And in general, visits do decrease the longer a person is in prison. Lack of visitations further isolates inmates who begin to believe their prison identity is all they have.

The outside roles of women as mothers/providers are quickly stripped away once they are inside the prison. (Jewkes 368-370; Goffman 10-11). Since approximately 77% of women serving time are mothers with primary custody prior to imprisonment, the separation from their children is often excruciating (Glaze and Maruschak). The loss of the identity of "mother" can be devastating to a prisoner. According to George, "The greatest casualties when we were incarcerated were our children and the reality is that if they don't have a strong network of support in place on the outside, there is very little we can do to protect them from the pressures they face" (110). Questions such as "will I see them again" or "what if they need me" haunt their existence. As women are generally the custodial parent, custody issues and children's living arrangements create fear and depression in female inmates.

Men face similar fears about their families. Concerns over how to be present in a child's life or how to provide for one's wife can be economically and emotionally destructive. Male prisoners have been known to divorce their wives to preempt the problems that come with having an imprisoned spouse, thus severing yet another emotional connection to the "outside world." They can become isolated and must rely on other prisoners for connection, a dangerous proposition in an atmosphere where no one is to be trusted. Developing emotional ties among prisoners is, however, a more common theme in the writings of women prisoners. George writes of "families" that develop in the prison and how the roles of mother, sister, daughter, and aunt are taken on by the inmates (101). These families provide a connection for the women that are beneficial in establishing identity as defined social roles and routines are assumed.

While there is little hope of release, LWOP prisoners will hold onto even the remotest possibility of getting out, as without hope life is bleak and often unbearable, as seen in the suicide of Hassine. Johnson and McGunigall-Smith argue that "Lifers do not adjust well because prison life is easy; they adjust well because self-interest moves them to make the most of a very difficult situation – a life confined to the barren, demeaning, and often dangerous world of the prison'" (qtd. In Leigey 14). Lifers can accumulate privileges over time, such as preferred work assignments, a single cell, or better access to phone calls and visits. Prisoners, therefore, are motivated to make a positive adjustment to make incarceration more tolerable. They often maintain excellent prison records in hope of early release, and many prisoners have established lifers' groups.

Not all prisoners are able to maintain their sanity when imprisoned for life. Writings by prisoners such as Hassine talk of "prison crazy," where the person can no longer live as defined by the prison, and his own fight for identity falls into the world of mental illness. Hassine tells the story of Kareem, another long-termer, who is suddenly hit with "prison crazy." Kareem explains to Hassine,

> "You know what's the most amazing thing about all this?" He suddenly took on the animation of a child, eager to share a secret. "The way it just kind of crept up on me. One minute I was normal, the next minute I was bugging out in my cell, talking to myself. I didn't know going crazy could snatch me from behind like that." . . . Kareem's last words echoed back to me: "nobody deserves to be treated like this. They might as well have killed me" (Hassine 30-31). [5]

The preference of death over life in prison is a theme that echoes throughout LWOP writing and in Hassine's choice to end his own life.

Assaults on the self leading to a suicidal state include a lack of privacy, lack of regular contact with sympathetic others, and damage to sexual orientation (Irwin and Owen 101-104). Space for mental and physical quiet time or thought is "subject to frequent violent intrusion," and the

---

[5] Hassine does not explain what happens to Kareem, so the reader is left not knowing his fate.

ability to find privacy implies a control over their environment that prisoners are lacking. Overcrowding in prison has become the norm; therefore, inmates are never alone once inside the prison. Hassine confirms "one of the cruelest aspects of a penitentiary is the way it leaves one isolated and lonely despite the overcrowded...surroundings" (77).

An assault on the prisoner's bodies can be equally intrusive, as evidenced by the health care provided. Maintaining good health is often impossible as there is a high incidence of contagious diseases, poor access to health care, overcrowding, poor hygiene, and inadequate and unhealthy food (Irwin and Owen 95-96; Heather 378-86). Admission to medical care costs anywhere from $5-15 a visit and must be paid in advance by the prisoners out of their commissary account with no guarantee of being seen soon. Treatment of chronic conditions such as diabetes, arthritis, or high blood pressure is difficult due to prescriptions not being filled on schedule (George 136, Hassine 84-91). "Just from the increasing size of medication lines and the growing number of inmates doing the brake-fluid shuffle, I have observed that psychotropic medications (also known as 'chemical shackles') are defining the behavior of an increasing percentage of inmates in the general population" Hassine reports (90). Prisoners often claim the best way to get into the infirmary is to be severely beaten.

There are, however, positive happenings in prison healthcare in the form of inmate volunteers. Many times, lifers become hospice workers or work the suicide watch units, as Robert Kelsey relates in his short story "Suicide!" This work allows for an otherwise impossible opportunity for prisoners to offer and experience emotional connection and physical support (Jervis). Service can come in many forms and be an avenue to creating a sense of identity. LWOP prisoners often serve as mentors (officially and unofficially), tutors, teachers, and even guide dog trainers. George writes of sharing her experiences training dogs with her children as a way to break the ice during visitation (107). They do so in an effort to give something back to other individuals in prison, share knowledge, and make amends in the only way available to them. In doing so, these women and men create intellectual and emotional relationships that support their identity as valuable individuals.

The published writing of prisoners reveals a world at odds with the idea that adaptation equals identity. Prison literature makes clear that injustice, dehumanization, and abuse are very much prevalent in prisons in America and worldwide. Having recently become more accepted by mainstream audiences, the writings are now gaining a larger readership. However, Americans are still hesitant to look behind prison walls, and the government, especially prison administration, does not encourage access to prisons. The literature is a call to witness the pain society condones as fair punishment and the destructive nature of the prison process. Since American taxpayers fund prisons, society has the right and the responsibility to explore the many truths behind the walls and the barbed wire, which can be accomplished in part through listening to the voices coming from behind the walls.

Works Cited

Abramsky, Sarah. "Lifers." *Legal Affairs.* March-April 2004. Web.

Abu-Jamal, Mumia. *Live From Death Row.* Reading, MA: Addison-Wesley, 1995. Print.

Blaze, Lauren E. and Laura M. Maruschak. "Parents in Prison and Their Minor Children."

Bureau of Justice Statistics. August 2008. Web

Bunyan, Scott. "The Space of Prison: The Last Bastion of Morality?" *Prose and Cons: Essays on Prison Literature in the United States.* Ed. D. Quentin Miller. Jefferson, NC: McFarland, 2005. 174-202. Print.

Carceral. K.C. *Prison, Inc.: A Convict Exposes Life inside a Private Prison.* Ed. Thomas Bernard. New York: New York UP, 2005. Print.

Chevigny, Bell Gale. "'All I have, a Lament and a Boast': Why Prisoners Write." *Prose and Cons: Essays on Prison Literature in the United States.* Ed. D. Quentin Miller. Jefferson, NC: McFarland, 2005. 1-11. Print.

Cunningham, Mark D., and Jon R. Sorensen. "Nothing to Lose? A Comparative Examination of Prison Misconduct Rates Among Life-Without-parole and other Long-Term High-Security Inmates." *Criminal Justice and Behavior* 33.6 (2006): 683-705. Print.

Dobrzanska, Ania, and Robert Johnson. "Mature Coping Among Life-Sentenced Inmates: An Exploratory Study of Adjustment Dynamics." *Corrections Compendium* 30.6 (2005): 8-. Print.

Flanagan, T.J. "An American Portrait Long-term Imprisonment." Ed. T. J. Flanagan. *Long-term Imprisonments: Policy, Science, and Correctional Practice. .* Thousand Oaks, CA: Sage. 1995. 10-21. Print.

Foucault, Michel. *Discipline & Punish: The Birth of the Prison.* New York, NY: Vintage Books, 1998. Print.

Franklin, H. Bruce, ed. *Prison Writing in 20th-Century America.* New York, NY: Penguin, 1998. Print.

George, Erin. *A Woman Doing Life: Notes from a Prison for Women.* Ed. Robert Johnson. New York: Oxford UP, 2010. Print.

Goffman, Irving. *Asylums: Essays on the Social Situation of Mental Patients and Other Inmates.* New York: Anchor, 1961. Print.

Gomaa, Sally. "Writing to "Virtuous" and "Gentle" Readers: The Problem of Pain in Harriet Jacob's *Incidents* and Harriet Wilson's *Sketches." African American Review* 3.2-3. 2009. 371-381. Print.

Haney, Craig. "The Contextual Revolution in Psychology and the Question of Prison Effects." *The Effects of Imprisonment.* Ed. Allison Liebling and Sahdd Maruna. UK: Willan, 2005. 66-93. Print.

Hassine, V. *Life Without Parole: Living in Prison Today.* Fourth Ed. New York: Oxford UP. 2009. Print.

Heather, Nick. "Personal Illness in Lifers and the Effects of Long-Term Indeterminate Sentences." *British Journal of Criminology* 17.4 (1977): 78-386. Print.

Irwin, John, and Barbara Owen. "Harm and the Contemporary Prison." *The Effects of Imprisonment.* Ed. Allison Liebling and Shadd Maruna. UK: Willan, 2005. 94-117. Print.

Jervis, Rick. "Inmates help in prison hospices." *USA Today* n.d.: *Academic Search Premier.* Web.

Jewkes, Yvonne. "Loss, Liminality and the Life Sentence: Managing Identity Through a Disrupted Lifecourse." *The Effects of Imprisonment.* Ed. Allison Liebling and Shadd Maruna. UK: Willan, 2005. 366-388. Print.

Kelsey, Robert. "Suicide!" *Doing Time: 25 Years of Prison Writing.* Ed. Bell Gale Chevigny. New York: Arcade. 1999. 86-96.Print.

Leigey, Margaret E. *Life Without Parole: A review of the Literature and Directions for Future Research.* National Criminal Justice Reference Service. NJC number 233835. 2010. Web.

Lopez, Tiffany Ana. "Critical Witnessing in Latina/o and African American Prison Narratives." *Prose and Cons: Essays on Prison Literature in the United States.* Ed. D. Quentin Miller. Jefferson, NC: McFarland. 2005. 62-77. Print.

Mauer, Marc, Ryan S. King, and Malcolm C. Young. "The Meaning of 'Life': Long Prison Sentences in Context." *The Sentencing Project.* Washington D. C. May, 2004. Print

MacKenzie, Doris, and Lynne Goodstein. "Long-Term Incarceration Impacts and Characteristics of Long-Term Offenders: An Empirical Analysis." *Criminal Justice and Behavior* 12.4 (1985): 395-414. Print.

MacKenzie, Doris, James W. Robinson, and Carol S. Campbell. "Long-Term incarceration of Female Offenders: Prison Adjustment and Coping." *Criminal Justice and Behavior* 16.2 (1989): 223-238. Print.

McConnel, Patricia. *Sing Soft, Sing Loud.* Flagstaff, AZ: Logoria, 1995. Print.

Nellis, Ashley and Ryan S. King. No Exit: The Expand Use of Life Sentences in America. The Sentencing Project. July, 2009. Web.

Norton, Judee "Norton #59900." *Doing Time: 25 Years of Prison Writing.* Ed. Bell Gale Chevigny. New York: Arcade. 1999. 228-235. Print.

Peck, Dennis. "Religious Conviction, Coping, and Hope: The Relation Between a Functional Corrector and a Future Prospect Among Life Without Parole Inmates." *Case Analysis in Social Science and Social Therapy.* 2:3, 1988, 201-219.

Riley Fast, Robin. "*Brothers and Keepers* and the Tradition of the Slave Narrative." *Mellis* 22.4. 1997. 3-20. Print.

Scheffler, Judith. "Imprisoned Mothers and Sisters: Dealing with Loss Through Writing and Solidarity." *Prose and Cons: Essays on Prison Literature in the United States.* Ed. D. Quentin Miller. Jefferson, NC: McFarland, 2005. 111 - 131. Print.

Soering, Jens. "The Story of Liam Q.: Life Without Parole." *Christian Century* 2008. 28-31. Print.

Sorensen, Jon, and Robert Wrinkle. "No Hope for Parole: Disciplinary Infractions Among Death-Sentenced and Life-Without-Parole Inmates." *Criminal Justice and Behavior* 23.4 (1996): 542-552. Print.

Sorensen, Jon, and Robert Wrinkle. "Patterns Of Rule-Violating Behaviors And Adjustment To Incarceration Among Murderers." *Prison Journal* 78.3 (1998): 222. *Academic Search Premier.* Web. 7 Aug. 2012.

U.S. Department of Justice. *Correctional Population in the United States, 2011.* December 2012.Web.

U.S. Department of Justice. *Prisoners in 2011.* December 2012. Web.

Wideman, John. *Brothers and Keepers.* New York: Mariner. 2005. Print.

Wormith, J. Stephen. "The Controversy Over the Effects of Long-Term Incarceration." *Canadian Criminology* 26 (1984): 423-437. Print.

Zamble, Edward. "Behavior and Adaptation in Long-Term Prison Inmates: Descriptive Longitudinal Results." *Criminal Justice and Behavior* 19.4 (1992): 409-424. Print.

CONTRIBUTORS

Melissa Ames is an Assistant Professor & the Director of English Education at Eastern Illinois University specializing in media studies, television scholarship, popular culture, and feminist theory. She teaches courses in these fields, as well as in composition and English education. Her work has been published in a variety of anthologies and journals, ranging in topic from Television Study, New Media, and Fandom to American Literature and Feminist Art. Her most recent publications include her books, *Women and Language: Essays on Gendered Communication Across Media* (2011), *Time in Television Narrative: Exploring Temporality in 21ˢᵗ Century Programming* (2012); chapters in *Grace Under Pressure: Grey's Anatomy Uncovered* (2008), *Writing the Digital Generation* (2010), and *Bitten by Twilight: Youth Culture, Media, and the Twilight Saga* (2010); and articles in the *Journal of Popular Culture* (forthcoming, 2014) and the *Journal of Dracula Studies* (2010).

Adrienne Bliss is an Assistant Professor of English in the Writing Program at Ball State University. Research interests and past presentations include the Grotesque, Trauma, and Prison Literature.

Mary Catherine Harper is a Professor and McCann Chair in the Humanities at Defiance College in Ohio, where she teaches literature and creative writing. She received her Ph.D. in literary criticism and theory and, also, creative writing at Bowling Green State University and her undergraduate degree at Montana State University. Her creative projects include both poetry and website visuals, and she explores the intertextuality of various literatures, the visual arts, cultural representations, and the philosophical Sublime. She has publications in *Studies in Indian American Literatures*, *Science Fiction Studies*, *Extrapolation*, *FemSpec*, *The New York Review of Science Fiction*. Harper also has publications in poetry magazines and has won the 2013 Gwendolyn Brooks Poetry Prize.

Rachel Herzl-Betz is a Ph.D. candidate in the University of Wisconsin-Madison Department of Literary Studies. Her research centers on the intersection between nineteenth-century British prose, rhetorical theory, and disability studies. Most recently, *Dickens Quarterly* published her essay on postal and print violation in Charles Dickens's novels, letters, and journalistic prose, entitled "Reading England's Mail: Mid-Century Appropriation and Charles Dickens's Traveling Texts."

Sarah Himsel Burcon is a Lecturer I in the Program for Technical Communication in the Engineering Department at the University of Michigan in Ann Arbor. She received her Ph.D. in American Literature and specializes in technical communication, feminist theory, American Literature, popular culture, and linguistics. She has published in anthologies and encyclopedias, and her most recent publications include her co-edited book, *Women and Language: Essays on Gendered Communication Across Media* (2011); chapters in *Time in Television Narrative: Exploring Temporality in 21ˢᵗ Century Programming* (2012) and *Revisiting the Past through Rhetorics of Memory and Amnesia* (2011); and articles for *Women and Popular Culture Encyclopedia (2013).*

Mandy Chi Man Lo is a Masters student at the University of Macau, majoring in English studies. She was awarded a full postgraduate studentship from the University of Macau and acted as a Teaching Assistant from 2011-2012. She was sponsored by the University of Macau to act as a Visiting Student Researcher in the Department of English at the University of California, Berkeley in America from 2012-2013. Ms. Lo was awarded several prizes and scholarships including the Wu's Group Academic Prize in 2010, the HSBC Scholarship in 2008, and the Henry Fok Foundation Scholarship in 2007.

Kristi McDuffie is a Ph.D. Candidate in English Studies at Illinois State University in Normal, Illinois. Her primary research interests focus on rhetorics of race in online environments, and her corresponding interests include digital literacies, critical pedagogies, and feminist rhetorics.

Matthew J. Sherman has a Master's Degree in German Studies from Michigan State University. He is currently a postgraduate student at the University of Oxford. His primary interests fall within the domain of Austrian Studies.

Emily J. Workman Keller is a Ph.D. student and Teaching Assistant at Marquette University. Emily's areas of interest include early 19ᵗʰ century British literature and John Milton, toward which she typically employs a combination of postcolonial and feminist theoretical approaches. Before beginning her studies at Marquette, Emily earned a Bachelor of Arts in

English from Westminster College of Salt Lake City, where she served as Editor-in-Chief of *Ellipsis...Literature and Art*. More recently, Emily earned a Master of Arts in English from Brooklyn College (CUNY). Emily has also earned a Master of Arts in Teaching Secondary English from Northeastern University and has taught high school English at Norwell High School in Massachusetts.